An Ordinary Doctor

An Ordinary Doctor

General Practice & Beyond

SUSIE WEST

First published in Great Britain in 2022 by West Jolly Books

Copyright © Susie West 2022

Edited, designed and produced by Tandem Publishing
http://tandempublishing.yolasite.com

ISBN: 978-1-3999-2703-1

10 9 8 7 6 5 4 3 2 1

A CIP catalogue record for this book is available from the British Library.

Printed and bound in Great Britain by CPI Group (UK) Ltd, Croydon CR0 4YY.

To my dearest twin sister Judy, without whom my life would have been so different.

~

A proportion of any profits from this book will go to:
Royal Medical Benevolent Fund
The South Atlantic Medal Association
The Middlesex Hospital Bursary Scheme
The Royal British Legion

PROLOGUE

As a doctor, dealing with the dead is something you have to get used to. Death is an unavoidable part of any medical career. But my first encounter with a dead body came many years before I became a doctor. It was my father's.

I was fourteen years old. It was a rainy Monday afternoon in late November in East London, and my father had died three days earlier, at the age of fifty-two, of a heart attack. The funeral director came to our home and collected my mother, my sister Penny and me, and drove us to the undertakers in Walthamstow. After about ten minutes of a silent journey, he stopped the car, and we followed him towards what looked like a shop. Inside, I have an overriding memory of dark wood floors and stained-glass partitions. Another undertaker, clad in a sombre suit, who had clearly been waiting for us, stood to greet us. He led us into a room at the back of the building, and there, lying in a wooden coffin, was my father.

I approached slowly until I was close enough to touch him. Only his head was visible. His hair had been brushed. I leaned forward and kissed his forehead, shockingly cold against my lips. I drew back and looked. He still had a small scratch on his face – he'd been gardening the weekend before. This seemed odd to me, that my father, now apparently dead, bore the marks from his recent living. I don't know what I had been expecting but I was surprised at how peaceful he looked. Until then, without really considering it, I had held blood and death to be synonymous. I had assumed that death would be messy. The last thing my father taught me was that it didn't have to be that way. He showed me it could be peaceful and calm and that a dead body was nothing to be afraid of. A valuable lesson for a future doctor.

The Coronation street party, 1953. Judy and me in
the foreground.

ONE

Medicine as a profession is often thought to run in families, and indeed there is truth in this. Some doctors come from long lines of medics stretching back generations. Their father and their father before that – rarely their mother until recent times – will have been a doctor, and so their destiny was decided before they knew it. Today, one in five medical students have at least one parent who is medically qualified.

But none of this was the case with me. Nobody in my family had ever been involved in medicine. I came from a family based in East London, a family of farm labourers, shopkeepers and butchers. My father was a travelling salesman and my mother, variously, a model, working in a greengrocer's, a housewife and eventually, many decades later, employed in the tax office. When I was growing up I didn't have so much as a second cousin or a distant aunt who was even a nurse, let alone a doctor. However, by the age of four I was bandaging anything that moved, and many things that didn't. My parents, my siblings, my teddy bear, any visiting guests – all were considered fair game for the attention of my novice nursing skills. Many Saturday mornings my father read the newspaper with one hand while I put his other arm into a sling.

Looking back from the distance of sixty years, I wonder what might have sparked this early interest in medicine. I am one of four girls, and was born in 1950, together with my twin sister Judy. I am the older twin by eleven very important minutes, and so the second youngest sister overall. My eldest sister, Penny, is three years older than me, and my next sister, Jan, is thirteen months older than me. For as long as I can remember, we were a close-knit group of four. However, while I have always been fortunate enough to enjoy good health, my twin sister Judy was not so lucky. From the age of seven or eight, she suffered from rheumatic fever and a number of complications that brought a new regular visitor to our house. A visitor we called Doctor Mac, short for MacKenzie-Brown, carrying a large black leather bag, with a calm, authoritative manner and a friendly face.

This was the era when doctors routinely made house visits, and during Judy's illness Doctor Mac would walk the four minutes it took to get to our house from his surgery. He would greet my mother cordially but formally, before proceeding upstairs to our bedroom to examine my twin sister, the patient. He was a modern doctor in his outlook, and thought Judy was better off nursed at home, rather than in hospital, where she would have been confined to bed totally immobile to protect her heart. I considered his visits exciting, viewing them as something very special. They also involved hushed conversations between adults in the hallway, and even as a very young child I sensed that the adults were worried by Judy's illness. So while I didn't understand what was happening, or what exactly was wrong with my twin sister, perhaps I somehow absorbed the importance of being able to try and fix her. I also knew that our parents trusted Doctor Mac completely. They never questioned his advice or considered a second opinion.

Fortunately, many years later, by her mid-teens, Judy was restored to full health. But by then, for me, the die was cast. The excitement of those early and frequent visits by our family doctor, when I would try to glean what he did, was to grow into a fascination with all things medical. In turn this was to provide me with a career as a GP myself, treating patients for thirty years. It would take me to sea as a ship's doctor, and into a war zone thousands of miles from home; it was to involve me in family planning and abortion services and even take me to give evidence at the Old Bailey in my work as a forensic doctor; and it was to see me serve as a doctor in the Royal Naval Reserve for the best part of thirty years.

I was born in Chingford, East London, but spent the first five years of my life in Walthamstow, the neighbouring borough. My mother, capable and stylish, ran an orderly household. We were well behaved and expected to work hard. My father was fun and practical but would be away from home for a week or two at a time due to his job as a commercial traveller. Both my parents wanted the best for their four daughters in a way that was possibly rather progressive for the time. The 1950s was still very much the age of men, and women were only just starting to emerge into the workplace. Women who did work often would resign their jobs on marriage, the assumption being that their husband would take care of them. But my parents were not typical 1950s parents. We were not being prepared to be wives to imaginary husbands. They had a shared desire for us to have better, easier lives than they had.

They had, after all, just lived through the war, during which my father had been a gunner in the army, and my mother had worked in a greengrocer in central London, witnessing the destruction of the Blitz each day on her tube journey in and out of the heart of the capital. My parents married after the war ended. When I was born, rationing was still in evidence, and the National Health Service (NHS) just two years old. But no one spoke about the war. It was over, and it was not to be talked about. Life was to be lived looking forward, no glancing over the shoulder at the past.

Mother single-mindedly wanted for her daughters what she had been denied simply because she was female. Her father, my grandfather, had made her leave school at fourteen and get a job, because in his opinion educating girls was a waste of time. She had passed the eleven-plus to go to the grammar school, but he didn't allow her to take up the place. In those days, children didn't argue with their parents, but just did as they were told, and so my mother duly left school at fourteen and started work in a shop. As we were growing up, my mother told us how much that mattered to her. She had liked school, had enjoyed learning, and had understood that it was a path to a different way of life. She may not have been able to have it for herself, but she wanted that for us. She had ambitions for us all, to achieve more than she had, to do better. And that began with a well-run home and an expectation that we worked hard.

We knew from an early age that if we worked, we would pass the eleven-plus and go to a better school. On Saturdays and in the summer holidays, my father would expect us to learn six new words a day and he would test us on them. He would also test us on our times tables. We were so close in age that we could all join in and he made it quite fun. There was an atmosphere of everyone striving to get ahead. We were aware that we were learning for ourselves rather than to satisfy our parents. Private education or tutoring was out of the question, but this – homemade spelling tests, passing the eleven-plus – was framed as entirely possible and within our reach. Other children at school were sent to elocution lessons but we didn't need that. Mummy was in charge of our diction and saw to it that we all pronounced everything perfectly. Just like the Queen. No East End accents for us. Judy particularly thrived on this and was Mummy's second in command when it came to picking up dropped aitches. Penny did go to piano lessons for a while but the rest of us did not follow suit.

My father, Douglas, was one of eight children. All of his

siblings – Dolly, Wally, Sid, Madge, Kitty, Pat and Bert – lived locally, except for Dolly, who had moved to Southend. They all kept in touch, particularly at Christmas. Their father, John, was a butcher, born in 1890 and descended from a journeyman butcher. I never met him, and nor did my mother, but I remember my grandmother, Lilian, who lived out her widowhood spending a few months with each of her children. She is one of my earliest memories, together with the Queen's Coronation in 1953. At least I think I can remember that, or I may have adopted the memory from my older sister, added to by the black and white photographs that detail the party held in our street. Nanna West used to pinch my cheek and call me 'little pale face'. I can only ever remember her sitting in a chair. Every evening she would be given a glass of Guinness. She died in April 1964 in her seventies, but we were not taken to her funeral, something that strikes me as odd in hindsight.

On my mother's side, there was Samuel Dean, her father, and we all loved him dearly. Grandad Dean was a farm labourer and used to tell us stories about how he first went to work for tuppence an hour. He was born in Holloway, North London. Part of family lore is the fact that Grandad Dean 'married up'. We all had a very clear idea of what that meant. Grandad Dean married Gertrude Smith, the daughter of a music publisher, and part of a fairly wealthy and established family. The music publisher – Great Grandad Smith – was offered the chance to publish Elgar's 'Land of Hope and Glory', but he turned it down. He didn't think the tune would catch on. It was taken elsewhere and obviously he was proved very wrong. That was the biggest mistake Great Grandad Smith ever made, apparently. But he did publish some other fairly well-known music and there must have been successes, as the family had money. Grandad Dean didn't, and so Gertrude's parents disapproved of the match.

We don't know how they met but Grandad must have moved to Woodford to be near Gertrude's family. Later, Grandad Dean took on decorating and painting instead of farm labouring. What he most wanted was to be a policeman, but that wasn't an option as he had lost his toes in the First World War and couldn't pass the medical. My mother Lilian (who my father always called Lee since his own mother was also called Lilian), was their first-born, and they also had a son, Len, who was in the Navy. But Uncle Len was frowned upon, because he married an Irish woman who was a single mother with a daughter. They went on to have three more daughters. We did see them from time to time, but Grandad Dean and Gertrude were shocked by his marriage, something that we were always aware of. In fact Nanna never got over this. The first daughter was always considered illegitimate and treated very differently to our real cousins.

As we were growing up, we were not aware that our parents' marriage also had a secret. Shortly after our father's death, when our mother was at work, I was looking for my birth certificate, and came across my parents' marriage certificate. It registered my father as divorced. I remember feeling shocked to the core by this discovery. Years later, I asked my Auntie Kitty about it, and she told me it was all rather hush-hush, that my father had indeed been married before, during the war, and that our mother was his second wife. Perhaps even more shocking, he had had a son with this first wife, whom we also knew absolutely nothing about. Thinking about it now, my father's first marriage occurred in wartime, when daily life must have often felt as if it were hanging by a thread, and so many people took decisions that they might not have made in peacetime. Many years later, we asked our mother about the marriage, and she told us what she knew ... which didn't amount to much. She was adamant that she had not been involved in the breakup of the marriage, although our parents had known each other for seven years before they married in 1947. Apparently they had been introduced by Daddy's brother Uncle Sid. While there may have been some overlap in terms of acquaintance, I feel certain, knowing my mother, that it is very unlikely she had an affair with him while he was married. It is interesting, though, how easily we four girls let go of the mystery that was our half-brother. We didn't dwell on his existence, or try to find him, which I suppose we might have. I asked my mother a few questions about him and she was not forthcoming in her answers.

Grandad and Nanna Dean loved our father a great deal. They would probably have known about his first marriage, but he must have won them over, as he did our mother. He was welcomed into the family in a way that Uncle Len's wife was not. But it was a different age. People didn't talk about things in the same way we do today. Things that were private or considered shameful stayed private or buried at all costs. The end result of this is that we never met our half-brother and, as far as I'm aware, my father lost all contact with him before he married my mother. Occasionally, I wonder now what he might have been like. I wonder if he is still alive. But some things are too late to follow up on, and best left in the times they came from. There is no point dragging them into the glare of the 21ˢᵗ century with its very different values and mind-set. It can't have been easy living in such socially constrained times, and fundamentally my parents were decent, loving people who behaved as was deemed appropriate at the time.

However, with the war consigned to the past and never talked about, the social landscape was starting to change. For a start, the size of the average family altered in a generation. While my father was one of eight, by the time I went to school, a family with four children, as we were, was considered a large family. Apart from my friend Betty, who was also one of four, most families were smaller. There may have been many reasons for this: the decline in church attendance; women getting better access to contraception, although the contraceptive pill was still twenty years away; more opportunities for women to live lives that didn't involve 'just' being a housewife; and a less rigid social order. Certainly for women, the potential benefits of these changes were significant, and, for a household of four young girls, came just in time.

Four girls spaced just three years apart was quite a handful. Once my mother told us that she had wanted six boys. But our parents embraced having daughters from the outset and worked to ensure we all developed our individual passions. They gave us a drive and a sense we could get out into the world and do anything we liked, if we worked hard. This approach paid dividends. With their encouragement, we all found our own interests, in a way still reflected in the lives we live today. Penny liked music, Jan loved horses, Judy was academic and wanted to be a teacher, and I loved everything to do with medicine. By the age of eight, I had declared my firm intention to be a nurse.

My father serving tea in our garden in Chingford, with me sitting on one of the garden hammocks that he sold.

TWO

My father explored a couple of career options before he settled on being a travelling salesman. Coming from a line of butchers, trying out the family trade was part of growing up, but quickly he discovered it wasn't for him. He then trained as a tailor, although I never saw him sew so much as a button on. Teaching us girls to sew was firmly left to my mother, to the point that we used to wonder if he were joking when he told us he had once been a tailor. He offered the fact that he always kept a pin behind his lapel as evidence. I was only really convinced when Auntie Kitty confirmed the story long after his death. Certainly, to me, my father was always a salesman, and during the week, while my mother ran the home, he would set off on his sales trips in his car, his wares in the boot, and be gone for some days.

He worked for a small company, James R Mace, selling umbrellas and garden furniture and walking sticks. He would drive around the country at a time when there were not yet any motorways, visiting department stores and shops, setting up accounts and demonstrating the goods he was promoting. He was well liked and obviously good at his job, because in 1955 we were able to move from Walthamstow to Chingford. The two boroughs were not far apart, but Chingford was where some of my father's family lived, and the nicer of the two. Chingford is on the edge of Epping Forest and is a perfect place for a growing family. It also offered us better grammar schools.

The new house, which my parents bought, was bigger than our old, terraced house. Judy and I still shared a bedroom but now we had a bed each. There was no central heating and in winter mornings it was freezing. I remember ice on the inside of the windows. My mother lit the boiler first thing in the morning, and we all got dressed in front of a two-bar electric fire. (Central heating wasn't common until 1970.) However, the kitchen was equipped with gadgets that were starting to become widely available. There was a fridge as well as labour-saving devices like a twin tub for washing and spin-drying clothes and an electric iron. I remember my mother getting a vacuum cleaner. All these mod cons were novel at the time. Nanna and Grandad used a boiler, a scrubbing board and a mangle to wring the clothes. They also had an outside toilet.

These new inventions came about as the factories that had built munitions for six years changed to the manufacture of things more suitable for peacetime living. The result was to make the housewife's life easier.

We had more space, including a morning room, a dining

room and a lounge, as well as a kitchen, four bedrooms and a bathroom. Penny had the best of the three smaller bedrooms with a lovely bay window overlooking the garden.

My father embarked on various DIY projects to improve the house still further. He was an early enthusiast for the knocked-through living space. I remember him taking a hammer to the dining room wall, knocking through a hatch and installing sliding reeded-glass windows. He was so pleased with it, he made a second one from the morning room through to the lounge. Whether my mother was consulted we were not aware. He mowed the lawn regularly, once a week in the summer, and laid out crazy paving at the front. My mother, meanwhile, took on the garden, and spent many a weekend planting and weeding. Our father would help with the flowerbeds but he always deferred to our mother as to what was a weed or not. Mother cooked very traditional 'meat-and-two-veg' meals, with few herbs and spices.

Food must still have been relatively scarce after the war, but we were not aware of that as we grew up. Certainly there was never any waste. The Sunday roast became shepherd's pie on a Monday night, and soup on Tuesday. We sometimes had a teatime treat called 'Auntie Gertie', which was white bread buttered by my mother with a layer of sugar on top. To make 'Auntie Gertie', sugar was poured onto a plate. Then the bread was pressed, butter-side down, onto the plate. How much sugar stuck depended on how thick the butter was and how hard you pressed. Food remained traditional in my early years. I never had rice, other than in rice pudding, until I was about to leave school. Rice was never part of a savoury dish and no one we knew ate pasta. The notion of any carbohydrate on the plate other than some form of potato was unheard of. Potatoes were versatile, they could be mashed or roasted or fried. But over the years, slowly, our diet began to change. The first curry we ever had was out of a packet; Vesta Curry was similar to a ration pack dried meal. We may have tried it as our Uncle Bert worked for Swiss Knorr and he was selling them. I remember the day the milkman started selling a new thing called yoghurt. The Milk Marketing Board had far too much milk and was looking for new things to do with it. Yoghurt proved a solution.

The wind of change was definitely about in some aspects of life. Yet in my parents' marriage, roles remained stereotypical. I never once saw my father cook so much as an egg. What is clear to me is that my parents really loved each other; they got on with each other, and with life, and with bringing up their four daughters. There were differences of opinion and occasionally big rows. Daddy was skilled with words and fun, and Mummy adored him. They both smoked. Daddy occasionally smoked a pipe. Sometimes we were allowed to light Mummy's cigarette and pass it to her.

We played cards with them. Mummy was very good at cribbage and we practised mental arithmetic as we learnt how to score. Mummy was very quick at mental arithmetic. Daddy had an amazing memory for the cards as they were played. Once we were interrupted by a phone call. I took the opportunity to switch a card. But of course Daddy knew what I had done. The punishment was swift and painful. I never cheated at cards again.

With Daddy away Monday to Friday, our weeks were given over to school, homework and our respective activities. Mother didn't drive, so we would walk home from school or get the bus. I of course focused mainly on health and first aid. I was fascinated by the body, by people with illnesses or conditions that made them slightly different. What was it that made them like this? Why did they have this condition, and what could be done about it? At the age of eight I found an outlet for some of this curiosity by joining the Junior Red Cross. Conveniently there was a local unit just ten minutes' walk from where we lived. I think our GP suggested it on one of his visits to see Judy. From the outset, I was an absolutely devoted member. The Junior Red Cross was rather like the Brownies or the Scouts in that we all wore a uniform. We wore berets and ties and were given badges and awarded medals. I earned badges in subjects like First Aid, Accident Prevention, Health and Hygiene and Home Nursing. I still have the certificates. We also went on parades. I particularly remember doing this on Remembrance Day. Although at first I didn't understand why we had to march on Remembrance Day, I felt proud for doing so and for belonging to the Red Cross. I remained part of the unit until I left school at eighteen. It gave me huge opportunities and was very important to my development.

The Red Cross wasn't the only organisation in the medical field. I recall there was a subtle rivalry between the Red

Cross and St John Ambulance, but I considered the Red Cross superior. I knew it was international, and I'd heard the story of its founding in 1863 in Switzerland, by a man called Henri Dunant, after he had witnessed the suffering of casualties at the Battle of Solferino, fought in Italy in 1859. In 1908 it was awarded a royal charter. The Red Cross gave me many things that I wasn't getting at school – a sense of belonging and responsibility, and a belief in my abilities. And as I grew older, the opportunities it offered me changed. Around thirteen, I volunteered to help at a Dr Barnardo's home, which provided care for orphans. At a Dr Barnardo's home, the children were put into a house with 'house parents', along the lines of a boarding school. The one nearest me was in Woodford Bridge, about fifteen minutes' drive from our house, and Daddy would take me there on a Sunday afternoon. I would help with the smaller children, very much in the role of a big sister. I enjoyed doing it, and it gave me confidence in meeting new people. By this time, I was in charge of some of the Junior Red Cross members, and allowed to teach them first aid. I remember organising the younger children into platoons and getting them marching smartly round the building. I remember enjoying the disciplined side of things.

After her initial early illness of rheumatic fever, which can affect the heart, my sister Judy developed a complication called osteomyelitis. This is when bacteria lodges in the marrow of the bone and becomes a chronic bone infection. Judy suffered with this on and off for years. It was very unpleasant for her. It scarred an upper arm and leg, and every now and then required a hospital stay. Later, she had plastic surgery on the scars. I never remember worrying that she would die, but I do remember thinking she missed out on certain things, like learning to swim, because of it. As I grew older, I became more aware of the serious nature of her illness and how concerned our parents were. When I was thirteen, I found my father crying, the only time I ever saw him cry. Judy had just fallen ill again and he was devastated that she had relapsed. Clearly, living with a seriously unwell child was a strain for my parents, but it was something they usually kept from us. I now understand it must have affected me too, every time she went back into hospital, or had an operation. But even after years of living with her intermittent ill health, it didn't seem to worry me consciously at the time. I never remember thinking that I was going to lose my twin. I felt certain she was going to be all right.

But while I might not have been worrying about Judy's health, I do remember from the age of about ten starting to worry much more about my father's. Daddy was a heavy smoker, as many people were in those days, and drank alcohol. By his early fifties, he was on pills for his blood pressure, and was under Doctor Mac's care. There were no signs of him being actively unwell, but I worried about him nonetheless. My parents slept with their bedroom door open, and from the age of ten onwards I remember regularly tiptoeing into their bedroom in the middle of the night, to check he was still breathing. I did it so often I knew which floorboards creaked, and where to step to avoid making any noise. For some reason I didn't want to be caught in the act of this nocturnal sortie. I would always creep back to my bed, hugely relieved and reassured. My father was still breathing, his chest was going up and down, and unaware of having been monitored. I could relax and go back to sleep. All was well. He was still here.

Except, suddenly, he wasn't.

My parents outside our house in Chingford, about 1960.

THREE

One ordinary Monday morning in late November 1964, when I had just turned fourteen, my sisters and I got dressed, had breakfast, and set off to school as usual. We were all at the grammar school by now, and generally walked there together. We said goodbye to both of our parents, as Daddy was not away travelling, and set off into the chill November air. Half an hour later, Daddy had a heart attack at home.

My mother told us about it when we came home from school that day. He was upstairs in bed, resting, and we went upstairs to see him. Doctor Mac had been round and Mummy was caring for him. Although we were all very alarmed and concerned, we all assumed he would be all right. Each day that week, we carried on as normal, going to school, and then coming home to homework and tea and an update on our father's health. But on Thursday, Doctor Mac sent Daddy to hospital.

At various times in my life, I have kept a diary, and my

diary entries around this time, kept in tiny little leather-bound books, are revealing. On that day, I simply wrote: "Daddy taken to hospital. He is very ill."

The following day, once again we set off to school as usual. We were worried about Daddy, but I don't recall thinking he wasn't making a good recovery, despite the foreboding of my diary entry. We came home at the end of the day, and our mother was there waiting for us. She told us she had visited Daddy at Connaught Hospital, and said he seemed to be doing well. Reassured, we had some tea and settled to our homework. Around 6pm, the phone rang.

It was the hospital.

"I'm very sorry to tell you, Mrs West, but your husband died half an hour ago."

And just like that the world stopped turning. The hospital hadn't even asked my mother if she was sitting down. We were all absolutely stunned. The tea turned cold, the homework lay on the table unfinished. It didn't seem possible, but it was. It had happened. I remember we all gathered round Mummy at the bottom of the stairs.

The ward sister phoned back about fifteen minutes later, to go through the details.

With hindsight, it is likely that my father had known he was dying. My mother later told us he had said two things to her that afternoon that really stuck. He told her: "I still think you've got a beautiful pair of pins" and later added: "I'm sorry I won't see the girls grow up." Both, viewed after the event of his death, seem to imply a foreshadowing, a sense that he knew that he was not coming home. But had he been obviously close to death, the hospital would surely not have let Mummy leave him.

It was like a curtain coming down on an act. The first act of our lives, the last act of his. In a flash we went from being part of a large, loving family, held safe by my father's strong arms, to a family of five women, four of us still children. My mother, born in 1919, into a different age, had worked variously at a greengrocer's, at Bourne and Hollingsworth department store, and rather amazingly as a model, even appearing in an advert on the television on one occasion. But predominantly she had been a housewife, and now she was solely responsible for four dependent daughters. Of course many families had been through much worse. We had a nice house but we were not by any means affluent. We were rising beyond working class and striving to improve ourselves. My father's income was all that we had, and I know now that he didn't leave a pension. But I didn't even think about any of that at the age of fourteen. All I could think about was that my father was dead.

My diary read: "Daddy darling died in peace at 5.30pm. Can't express how we all feel."

I remember it was a terrible weekend.

Saturday's diary reads: "Utterly miserable."

On Monday, we all went back to school. Before we set off, our mother asked us if any of us wanted to see Daddy in the Chapel of Rest after school. I decided to go, and so did Penny. We went together and so it is that my father was the first dead body I ever saw. I remember thinking as I looked at him, waxy cheeks and closed eyes, that no dead body

I ever came across in my future career in medicine could possibly be worse than looking at his.

We went to school on Monday, Tuesday and Wednesday that week. Thursday was my father's funeral. The school had been informed.

"Daddy's funeral and cremation," I recorded. "Can't say anything."

The next day we went back to school again. I remember a teacher shouting at me for being absent the day before. I couldn't tell him I'd been at my father's funeral. I just froze. Inside I simmered, and felt furiously angry with the school for not showing more understanding.

At home, letters flooded in. I remember one neighbour wrote telling us "not to grieve, as it will only upset your mother". Others came from his work colleagues, people he had visited across the country on work trips, but whom we had never met. They all remembered him fondly. He had clearly been much liked and popular.

Immediately after my father was buried, we were facing the reality of the road ahead without him. The company he had worked for came and collected the car. Penny, at sixteen, wanted to leave school and get a job, to help with the family finances. But my mother absolutely refused to let her, and Penny's teacher backed her up, pointing out to Penny how close she was to finishing her O levels, which would in turn lead to a better job. I look back now at Mummy with total admiration. I think I only saw her cry once, after Daddy's funeral. She was very committed to holding life together for us. She had just lost her husband,

and I imagine she must have felt very apprehensive about how she would manage. But she was adamant that all of us would finish school, and that she would find a way to make this happen. And find a way she did.

She told us early on that an insurance policy had paid off the mortgage on the house, which meant we didn't have to move. But we still had no income. I think that Doctor Mac introduced Mummy to a tax inspector who lived round the corner. He suggested applying to become an assistant with the Inland Revenue, working in a tax office in Woodford. She applied and started almost immediately, earning enough to keep us all going through the final years of school.

I noted in my diary "Mummy has started her new job" and a few weeks later "Mummy really likes her job." She had taken to it so well, and some of those she met went on to become close family friends.

Janny did leave school at sixteen as she didn't like school at all. Initially she went to work at the Bank of England (which she didn't much like either; horses were her passion and she later got a job in a stables). Penny stayed through the sixth form, took her A levels and qualified as an occupational therapist. Judy and I took our A levels. The only subject we had in common was English. Judy was better at this than me, but both of us studying the same texts undoubtedly helped me. I was furious that she got a much better grade than me. Judy went on to train as a teacher. She had absolutely blossomed as a linguist since about the age of fifteen, when she met a French girl, Beatrice, who was staying in Chingford. They became firm friends and loved improving their language skills. Both were committed to teaching their own language to the other. Beatrice came to stay with our family and we all thrived on this international contact. We still remain in contact now. Mummy must have realised that foreign visitors were a good alternative to foreign holidays and an Italian and a German girl came later. I started nursing and ultimately had a career as a doctor. So our mother's determination to give us the future she never had, despite the death of our father, was her great achievement.

My mother was only forty-five when our father died. That is a young age to become a widow, and they had been married for only eighteen years. While she mourned and missed him, she never, as far as we know, attempted to replace him and never complained. Once she started the job at the tax office, she had to take the bus every day to Woodford. She had never learned to drive but now she decided she would. She took lessons, passed her test, and bought a car. From then on, she drove to the office. She was good at her job and enjoyed it. She went on courses and became a Tax Officer. To start with it was very much a desk job dealing with vast amounts of paperwork, but she really thrived when she was put on the public enquiry desk. She dealt with people patiently and sympathetically. She was very diligent and if a tax rebate were due she would ensure that it was paid. It was not unusual for her to come home with a bunch of flowers from a grateful taxpayer.

She worked until she was sixty-five, and then, when she retired, she started volunteering at the charity Arthritis

Care. There she quickly went onto the committee as social secretary, planning the programme and, before we knew it, she was the master of ceremonies at the social evenings. She had a talent with people. She also started to sing again. We always knew she had a lovely voice as she had sung to us when we were small. But now she would introduce the visiting guests and host the entire evening and lead the sing-alongs. She was an amazing role model for us all. She made a lovely home for us, friends always welcome, and we were comfortable with our home and family. In many ways, we were very rich indeed. Our school friends always said that our mother was lovely.

Still, the first few months after Daddy died were very hard and made harder by the level of denial around our grief that we collectively undertook. We all just bottled up our grief. Our father died in November. I felt that Judy was determined that we should not discuss it at school or tell our friends. I didn't even tell my best friend Betty, whom I'd known since the age of eleven, and am still friends with today. None of our friends had any idea that we had lost our father.

It was a case of stiff upper lip all the way. Now I know that is not the way to deal with death, particularly the first significant death a young person faces. But then I felt I had to follow Judy's line. So of course we all behaved a little oddly, and no one knew why. We were much more withdrawn, and rushed home at the end of each school day. Betty remembers that we were often a bit snappy and distant at times. I also remember that, as I was walking home each day, the word 'dead, dead, dead' would bounce round my head and I would think, *what does that actually mean?* The word 'dead' seemed to lose its meaning and yet it had changed my life.

Slowly, time passed. My New Year's Eve diary entry simply said: "Miss Daddy terribly."

Things only changed early the next term, when Judy became disproportionately upset over a tiny thing at school. Finally the awful news came out to everyone and we all had to start to face the fact that our father was dead. My diary shows that, on 26 January 1965, I finally told Betty and another friend, and became so distressed that I had to be taken to the medical room with a teacher. We had all been very ill-prepared for him to die. He had been only fifty-two. But at least the secret that I had felt so ashamed about had come out.

For a whole year after his death, I wouldn't let a day go by without thinking of him. I was frightened of *not* thinking about him, as if that would somehow diminish his memory. I didn't want to meet new people who had not known Daddy. Those who had known him somehow felt more important, even if I couldn't talk about him. I also tried to find him again, through religion, trying determinedly to believe in God. I read the Bible a lot and went to church. That made no difference. After a while, I stopped going to church and I began to face life without him, to accept it, and deal with it. That felt an essential shift – it was only then that any kind of healing process could begin. However, the connection with the church had the benefit of introducing us to a lot of young people. Penny met her future husband and I met my first serious boyfriend.

More than a year after my father died, I volunteered for what is now known as Mencap. I started to help at the local social club for people with learning disabilities (then known as mentally handicapped) on Friday nights. I would help the organisers to run the evening. I would chat to the club members, play games with the members or just be a friend to them. I did it because I thought it was a very good training ground for being a nurse. I knew I needed to be able to approach someone, introduce myself, say hello, look them in the eye, talk to the person rather than the disability. The Red Cross had given me a great deal, but I had not had much contact with those who had medical problems. My earlier volunteering had been to help a mother, Mrs B, who had a child aged about nine who could neither walk nor talk. I would take her out in a pram for about an hour at a time to give Mrs B a break. This was a hard and solitary task, but the Friday night club gave me a chance to meet people whom I hoped that, one day, I really would be able to help. I did it because I enjoyed it, but also because I had a clinical interest in each condition. While I made it my business to understand what they were saying, and enjoyed talking to them and being with them, I also wanted the medical details and I had an interest in understanding what the medical prognosis was. I was fascinated by the idea of a diagnosis.

My mother encouraged my involvement with this club, but I felt Judy disapproved of this development. She felt I should be studying harder, as it was the year before our O levels. She was working round the clock, unlike me who was going off every Friday night to the club. She knew I was having a good time. But it felt right for me. Some doctors – surprisingly – don't like the patient-facing side of medicine but I've always welcomed it, and I think my early experience at this club, as well as my later nursing experience, combined to make me a better practitioner overall. I met a young couple, then in their early twenties, at the club. They later married and I am still in touch with them today.

Through the Red Cross the opportunity came up to go to a residential camp as a helper of children with disabilities, and I jumped at the chance. Tiptree was about an hour and a half away from where we lived, and I went for two weeks in the summer before I was sixteen. My role was to help the children who came to the camp, which was in a school, to support them and to have fun with them. I was horrified to find that I felt terribly homesick at first, but soon I got over it and ended up really enjoying the two weeks there. During that time I met other like-minded teenagers, including a boy called Roger, who became the object of my first crush. We stayed in touch for a while after the trip, writing letters.

I remember coming home at the end of the trip, to a disapproving Judy, who was obviously going to do much better than me in her O levels at this rate, feeling tired but satisfied. My social circle was for the first time spreading beyond my cosy nest of family and school. I was starting to take small steps into the world I wanted to inhabit and making friends with people whose interests mirrored my own.

During the two weeks, all of us had also been assessed by the Red Cross leaders, who were looking for delegates to represent the Junior Red Cross at an international conference, to be held the following year. They monitored how confident we were, how well we mixed and whether we could speak up in a group. I didn't really understand the concept of being observed and assessed and I was so focused on the day-to-day job that I was not really aware it was happening. Next I was invited to go away for a weekend selection at Barnet Hill, which was a small stately home belonging to the Red Cross. I was thrilled to be in such an awe-inspiring setting, but also a bit daunted. To my delight I was selected to go to Austria to the International Red Cross conference, as a British representative of the Junior Red Cross.

This first foreign trip was very formative. I was away for about three weeks. We flew to Vienna and at first we stayed in a youth hostel. My diary entries from that time record how much I loved looking around Vienna. Then we were taken to Langenlois, which is in the Krems-Land in Lower Austria. We stayed at a place that was a farming school in winter and a hostel in the summer. It was a truly international conference: Austria, Germany, Sweden, Romania, Poland, Great Britain and Yugoslavia were represented, with the biggest delegation from Austria itself. Everything was new and fascinating. Even something as simple as drinking *apfelsaft* (apple juice) was novel, as I had never had anything other than water or tea. I carefully documented every detail. I realised there was a whole world out there to be discovered and I was absolutely thrilled about it. We went on walks up mountains and explored the countryside. I remember visiting vineyards. There were also early morning sports activities and each delegation had to produce a national themed entertainment for one evening of the stay. I ended up in charge of producing the British contribution. I noted in my diary how worried I was about the responsibility, but also recorded several days later how delighted I was that it went down wonderfully well. In the letters to my sister I noted down all the songs that I sang. We also did some Red Cross first aid activities, and an Austrian television station came to film us, which made us all feel very important. The whole event, with its various challenges and particularly meeting many other nationalities for the first time, really broadened my horizons. I also realised that my French was not that good and needed to improve, as even though there was no French delegation, at times French was the only common tongue. Even in 1967, many of the Eastern European countries spoke impressively good English.

I feel I owe the Junior Red Cross a great deal. The director of our local branch, Mrs Peake, who lived very near the unit, became something of a mentor. She knew I was going to become a nurse. I think I told everyone who would listen. Which meant that when, a few years later, I decided to leave nursing to go to university I felt really guilty. I worried that Mrs Peake would think less of me, reneging on my commitment. I didn't want to visit her and admit that

I had left, so I never saw her again. Decades on, I hope she would have understood.

Perhaps it was thanks to the Red Cross that my love of travel was ignited. We had never been abroad as a family. Later that year, I went to Italy, first to Milan, and then on to Bisceglie briefly as an au pair. I learnt some Italian, and improved my French, although fundamentally I am not a natural linguist.

My route over the next few years wasn't straightforward. Although I'd been committed to the idea of nursing, Doctor Mac had always told me I should aim higher, and be a doctor instead. Somehow I felt rather indignant that nursing should not be regarded as a high enough calling. In my teens I couldn't envisage becoming a doctor; apart from Doctor Mac I had no role model for that, and at that time not many women became doctors. So my focus remained very much on becoming a nurse. During my A level years I applied to do a four-year course that would qualify me as a Health Visitor, District Nurse and State Registered Nurse (SRN). The course was based at the Hammersmith Hospital, which I had heard was a very good hospital to train at. However, this reputation was based on its medical research rather than its nursing prowess, something I did not understand at the time. The decision seemed the right and obvious one, so in September 1969 I moved into the Nurses Home ready to start my new career. Judy had moved to Cambridge to study teaching and French and threw herself into the social life that she had been looking forward to. She had independence and enormous opportunities to make new friends. My twin and I were apart for long stretches, and that was a significant change in itself, and we were embarking on very distinct careers.

I loathed the Nurses Home from the outset. There were lots of rules about not having visitors and nothing resembling a social life. The group doing the four-year course was small, and there were only about fifteen of us. One of them persuaded me to join the Nurses Christian Fellowship, and she remains a lifelong friend. But overall, the experience was less than promising and I couldn't believe what I had chosen. My room overlooked 'D wing' of Wormwood Scrubs prison, which was utterly grey and depressing. We were told that the long-term prisoners were ogling the nurses. It didn't really matter whether that were true or not, the result was it made us feel extremely uncomfortable.

The course itself was well organised. After the initial 'block' of theoretical training and learning how to make beds we were sent to the wards. There we were part of the team looking after patients, with a senior nurse to supervise and teach. We were rotated through different departments so we would gain a broad range of experience. Even as a first-year nurse I worked with junior doctors, and one day I clearly recall telling the junior doctor what prescription he needed to write. I, as a nurse, could not write or sign it. I quickly realised that if I spent my life as a nurse telling a doctor what he needed to do it would be a very frustrating career. But at first I wasn't sure what to do about this realisation. During my first year, part of the course required me to spend half a term at the University of Surrey. I remember asking questions in lectures and the tutor would say "Don't worry, as a nurse you don't need to know that," and I would feel furious inside.

It was at this stage that I started seriously to think that, perhaps, I could be a doctor after all. I enjoyed the work with patients, but was concerned that I was not in the right place. It was a very confusing time, and I worried deeply about giving up. Even at nineteen I was someone who finishes what they start, but I couldn't shake the feeling that I was not going to be satisfied as a nurse. I loved the practical side, dealing with real people, with patients, and trying to help them, but I was feeling terribly limited by the things I wasn't allowed to do or learn. Penny helped me work through this dilemma and ultimately to reach the decision I did. She was by now studying to become an occupational therapist, and when I shared my feelings with her and told her I was thinking of leaving nursing and starting a degree instead, she encouraged me. She pointed out that I could always do a degree and then be a nurse afterwards, but that it was quite unlikely that I would become a nurse and go back and do a degree later. At the time there was not the array of academic options that exist today. The Open University didn't take its first students until 1971. Penny's logic made sense, so, troubled as I was by my situation, I left the Hammersmith and applied to do a degree in Biological Sciences at Bedford College, London University.

Even this felt uncertain. I spent the summer before I was due to take up my place wondering if I was still taking a wrong turn. A degree in Biology would not make me a doctor and, by now, that was what I felt I really wanted to be. However, to be a doctor I needed Chemistry A level, which I had chosen not to take. There wasn't much career advice around in those days, and so I was having to work out a way by myself. Looking back, if had I been correctly advised, I could have applied straight to medical school to do what was known as First MB for those with the wrong A levels to catch up. It was a pre-medical course which today might be described as an access course. This underlines the importance of accurate advice at these early crossroads in life. Actually my Biology teacher, Mr Boyce, had spotted that I was understanding scientific papers rather well when I was in the lower sixth and at the time had questioned if nursing were right for me. But neither of us had the knowledge of the system. We knew that my choice of English and Economics as my other A level subjects precluded the option of medicine at university, but neither of us had heard of First MB.

Nevertheless, in 1970 a degree in Botany and Zoology felt interesting, if not my first choice. I had applied very late in the year. As it happened Betty was going to read Physics at Bedford College, and that made the decision a bit easier. She was also a year later in applying, having worked for a year. One of the other prefects from school, the head boy, was already at Bedford, studying Sociology, and I met up with him to find out more about the college.

Bedford College had been a women's college before it started admitting a few men in 1965. By 1970 there were still far more female students than males. I am not really sure how much I was aware of this at the time, but it was situated in Regent's Park, which was beautiful and about as far a cry from Wormwood Scrubs as a London college could be. I was unsure if this was a good enough basis on which to accept the place I had been offered. I never discussed my dilemma with my mother. I knew that she was worried about me having 'dropped out' of nursing, but we were never able to discuss the pros and cons. Mother was always good at silent support. All the positives added up, and after a summer of deliberation, spent at home other than a brief spell as an au pair in France, I quashed the small voice inside me saying 'but you want to be a doctor' and took up my place to read Botany and Zoology.

THE MIDDLESEX HOSPITAL HOUSEMEN — AUTUMN 1978

1978: my first house job at the Middlesex Hospital.

FOUR

When I started at Bedford College I initially lived in halls of residence in Swiss Cottage. I liked the short commute each morning, as it made me feel part of the real world. I compared my choice with Judy's in Cambridge, and felt pleased with the decision I had made. Her life seemed to me a non-stop social whirl. While I could get the benefit of this if I wanted, by going to Cambridge for weekend visits, London felt the more adult place to be.

At Bedford, I was aware that the other students were from a wider spectrum than my peers on the nursing course. I met students from abroad, and others from more academic families than mine. One fellow student had a mother who was a biochemist. He told me that he had grown up with a chart of the Periodic Table pinned to a wall in the kitchen, and had had to learn it off by heart by the time he was ten. That made our family spelling test look rather modest. However, as undergraduates we were suddenly all equal despite our differences.

The college offered units or modules rather than a standard degree, which was innovative at the time. I was able to pick units that interested me, and that would prepare me should I decide to switch to medicine. Consequently I chose Biomathematics, Statistics and Chemistry, to fill the gaps that I knew existed in my knowledge and qualifications to date.

The hall of residence was run rather along the lines of a Cambridge college. We were expected to eat together in the dining room, with a member of the academic staff presiding at each table. We did have a kitchenette on each floor, but this was simply for making tea and toast. At the end of every term, we had to pack up our rooms, which felt very disruptive, and I didn't particularly enjoy that style of living. A natural solution arose to this problem at the end of my first year, when Penny got married and moved to Africa with her husband. They had been living in a flat on the second floor of a house in Highbury Hill, and I was allowed to take on their tenancy, at the cost of £1. 7s. 6d. per week. This gave me a settled base. I loved that first home of my own. I decorated it and stayed there for seven years. It had its own little kitchenette and sitting room, but I had to share a bathroom with the people downstairs. This wasn't ideal, but it was manageable, and I always took my wash bag with me when I went home for Sunday lunch, to make full use of my mother's hot water.

Socially I made good friends at Bedford, but I was also quite a serious student. I was elected onto the Student Union Executive as the Welfare Officer, and my early nursing experience made me quite suited to this task. I discovered ways in which students needed support, and also learned something about committee work. I became friends with some of the other students on the committee. I was still friends with Betty, but over time we were seeing less of each other. I would seek her out when I had a work problem I couldn't solve. Then I would visit her in her digs, close to Swiss Cottage. She taught me how to use a slide rule, which I had never got to grips with at school. But slowly our paths were diverging. She got married and went on to have children at a young age, while my determination to be a doctor was cementing. The start of my second year at Bedford College saw me applying to medical school. I was accepted by Middlesex Hospital which was just half a mile or so away across the Euston Road. It was a conditional offer and required me to achieve a 2.1 degree. I knew I needed to work very hard if I was going to get in, and was devastated when I got a 2.2. This only confirmed to me that I absolutely *had* to become a doctor. Despite my lower-class degree the Middlesex Hospital agreed to take me anyway. I was over the moon with joy and relief.

Having got into medical school, I had to address how to fund it. It was undoubtedly a very fortunate time to be a student in the UK, because full grants were available, dependent on parental income, and our mother had little to spare us. Tuition fees were paid by the Education Authority, irrespective of parental income. However, I had already had one grant from Waltham Forest, and it was by no means certain that I would get another, so I applied for a bursary to the Draper's Company. In the event, I gained both a grant by the Inner London Education Authority, as I had been a permanent resident by now in Highbury Hill for two years, and the bursary. I tried to return the bursary when I was awarded the grant, but the Draper's Company told me to keep it. An act of generosity which I always appreciated. Like many students, I also expected to do some part-time jobs, anything ranging from cleaning to auxiliary nursing, to help make ends meet. But it was and is important to get this balance right. Too much part-time work reduces the ability to study. I was already used to earning money as I'd had my first Saturday job at the age of sixteen in a tobacconist, earning one pound for a day's work, and had been financially independent since I had left home at eighteen. My early independence did me no harm, as all my small jobs gave me confidence in my abilities.

By September 1973, I was enrolled in medical school and starting my training as a doctor. This involved two years of theory followed by three years of clinical training, spent in a series of short appointments through the various departments of medicine. Five years in total followed by one year as a houseman covering six months of medicine and six months of surgery. I got no credit for my Biology degree, so there was a long road ahead. But I didn't feel daunted. Rather, I felt excited that I was finally on the right career path, and my first degree certainly helped me in some subjects, such as physiology.

My part-time work as an auxiliary nurse gave me some worthwhile hands-on medical and caring experience and, when I was training at medical school, it quickly became obvious that not all would-be doctors liked that aspect of the job. During my career I've lost count of the number of times I might see a patient look as if they are about to vomit and the doctor rushes for the door. I've always felt comfortable with that side of things. I also learned good communication skills. Having worked with elderly people or sick people as a nurse or a volunteer, I was used to the idea of approaching people who need help. Later, before we went on the wards in our third year, we were expected to work with the nurses on shifts for two weeks, to understand their job. I loved reverting to being a nurse, but many of the medical students did not like the 7.30am starts and being under the instruction of a ward sister.

When I was settled at medical school, I made contact with Doctor Mac again. I wanted to let him know that he had been right all along. He was still in the same practice where he had spent his whole career. We reconnected, and he was really pleased for me, and still determined that I should become a GP. His wife had already died, and sadly he fell ill while I was training. I went to visit him at the Royal London Hospital in Mile End. That felt very poignant, sitting by his bedside, offering him grapes, and he died before I qualified. Most people have one or two adults outside the immediate family who touch their lives, and he was one of the important people in mine.

Medical school after three years of undergraduate life at Bedford College had a very different feel to it. Most obviously, more than 90 per cent of the students were male.

Many of the students were also younger than me, having come straight from A levels. I fell in with a group of slightly older fellow graduates, all of whom had done a first degree in something other than medicine. One of them lived near me in Highbury and we helped each other a great deal through our exams. After the first two years of theory were completed, we started on the practical side, rotating through a number of different specialities, spending a few weeks at a time in each. We were put into firms, or groups, of six or eight students and did all our rotations in that group. The end result was that we formed a very tight circle. It was a wonderful system, as we were mutually supportive. We could cover for each other and teach each other if there were things we didn't understand. We rotated through several London hospitals and out to their satellite hospitals. I spent time at the Central Middlesex, at Park Royal and at Welwyn Hospital. There were links too with hospitals at Southend and Stoke. I had to pay my rent wherever I was based, so I did my best to avoid going too far away from London. But for some rotations we had to live in. One such was Obstetrics and Gynaecology, which took me to Welwyn in Hertfordshire. The rotation lasted six weeks, and I had to deliver at least twelve babies during that time. I think I delivered more than that; Obs. and Gynae. was to remain an area of enduring interest to me. My surgical house job took me back to London again to the Royal Northern Hospital on the Holloway Road, conveniently just up the road from my flat.

Since my early experience with the Red Cross in Austria, I

had discovered a love of travel. As a child, we had never gone on holiday, so my trips weren't really focused on leisure or going to a beach, but more on seeing something of a wider world. And they were usually combined with a medical aspect. At the end of my first year as a medical student, in 1974, I contacted a friend working abroad, and arranged to spend some weeks in South Africa and Botswana. I flew to Johannesburg – direct flights to South Africa had only just opened up – and Apartheid in all its awfulness was in full swing. I remember going to a bank to withdraw some money shortly after I arrived, and going in the wrong entrance, and lots of people saying no, no, and being told to leave and go to a different one. I was astonished that someone was expected to go in a different entrance because of the colour of their skin.

My friend was a geologist and we drove up through Botswana. His brother was a doctor working as the only surgeon in a mission hospital and I arranged to stay for a month with him. I worked in the outpatient section, talking to patients who came to the hospital, before they saw the doctor. The most common complaint they presented with was 'waist ache'. Trying to understand what they meant by this was a challenge, and highlighted to me the cultural aspects that could affect a medical practice. Sometimes it was simply a calling card, a way to get to see the doctor, and once there they would open up about what they really wanted help with. Alternatively, such a general description could turn out to be any number of conditions. At the same time I undertook a study on how illnesses could present differently in different cultural backgrounds. I didn't publish it but working at the mission hospital felt a perfect way to prepare for clinical practice. It also showed me what opportunities lay ahead.

In 1975, in my next year of training, an opportunity to choose an elective unit of ten weeks, which could be spent abroad, arose, and I seized it. I chose to go to India, to Calcutta Medical Hospital, in the Obstetrics and Gynaecology department. This was another hugely influential period, revealing a very different way of practising. Each day, about sixty women would be struggling to see the doctor. The doctor would select one of the patients through a system known only to him, sit them on a seat in front of him, and with all the other patients watching, proceed to examine her. Patients were treated impersonally and it felt fairly appalling. It really emphasised to me the importance of addressing the individual sensitively and in private. While I was there, I wrote a study on the termination of pregnancy. Women would walk ten miles to the clinic, and once they arrived, they didn't expect any discussion about why they couldn't continue with the pregnancy. They simply climbed onto the couch, had the termination and then walked home again. It was horrifying and hard, and rather extraordinary to witness the bravery of these women, who for various reasons – most likely, lack of food and money, and thinking of the children they already had – knew they simply could not manage another child. This experience was to shape me, and in my later career I was regularly to work shifts at a women's clinic in London. It cemented my belief that women really need to be in charge of their own bodies. It also gave me a lasting respect for the training that the medical students received in Calcutta, easily comparable to my own.

Combining travel and work was to remain attractive to me. A few years later, when I had qualified and was working as a junior doctor in the Middlesex Hospital, I saw an advertisement for a medical escort, who was required to accompany a sick patient from London to Los Angeles. Reading it, I thought "I can do that." Rather boldly, I asked my consultant if I could have a few days off to do it, and I think he was so surprised that a junior doctor dared to ask him anything at all directly that he said yes. Within a few days I found myself on a paid-for flight to LA.

I was delighted to think that now as a qualified doctor doors would open for me. It seemed a wonderful idea to travel the world using my qualification. I still had my time as a junior doctor to complete, and the difficult decision to make of what area of medicine I would choose to work in. While I liked obstetrics and gynaecology, as a relatively mature student, a decision to pursue this felt problematic. As I neared the end of my training, in 1978, I was already twenty-seven years old. If I specialised in gynaecology, I wouldn't qualify as a consultant until my mid to late thirties. This seemed far too old to be embarking on what would effectively be the start of my career. I had also worked out by now, after years of night shifts, that I needed my sleep. I did not thrive with irregular sleep patterns, as some of my fellow students seemed to. So my thoughts turned instead to something that could be mostly done in daylight hours, with a more structured work schedule. Doctor Mac's kind face swam into view and general practice seemed the obvious answer. He had been right all along.

General practice is an interesting area of medicine. It is a vital medical service, but it has also been somewhat looked down on by other doctors. Many GPs themselves have a chip on their shoulder about it. When I told one of the consultants I was thinking about general practice, he told me I should be "aiming higher". Yet a GP is usually the first point of contact for someone who is unwell. GPs need to be highly qualified and decisive. In short appointment times – much shorter today, at under ten minutes, than when I started – they need to be able to decide whether the person in front of them has a self-limiting illness, one that will essentially clear up on its own; something that they can treat with a prescription; or something that needs to be referred to a specialist for further investigation. To make those kinds of decisions, they need a solid bedrock of medical knowledge, an ability to listen to the patient as they explain how they feel and what their symptoms are, and a decisive mind. All this felt like a good fit. I had learned early to evaluate the patient in front of me, from my first experiences with Mencap and in nursing. I still had an enduring interest in diagnosis, and decision-making was rarely a problem. To qualify as a GP required me to undertake twelve months in supervised general practice. The more I thought things through, the more my sense grew that this was the right speciality for me. There was a relatively short training period, and progress to partnership was almost guaranteed. Although at that point I had no plans to get married and have children, I felt that I was probably conventional enough to want to do so one day. I also knew with absolute clarity that, if I did have a family, I would always continue with my profession. General practice was the obvious choice when it came to having a family and continuing to work.

But first, I had to pass my final medical exams. I remember very clearly the day I went to get the results. It was the summer of 1978. The results were posted up on the notice board outside the refectory, and it was utterly nerve-racking. My sister Judy had come to be with me, to share the news. I remember going down the stairs to the board and looking to find my name on the list. I felt my breathing stop while my eyes scanned the list. And lo! My name was there. I was ecstatic. Similarly, all around me candidates were erupting into screams or bursting into sobs of elation. It had been a long road to qualification, and at times it had seemed that 1978 was a year that would never come. But it had.

I was finally a doctor, which was, and is still, quite a dramatic watershed in a person's life. Overnight you go from being a student, who from society's point of view is nothing much at all and fairly far down the pecking order in life, to a qualified doctor, and so a cog in a great and respected wheel, and something slightly different from lay society and even from your own family. From the moment I qualified I just *felt* different. For some of my fellow students, whose parents were doctors, or had been researchers or famous consultants, this was just the first expected step and perhaps not such a big deal. But for me qualification was not just the beginning of a career; it also felt like a pinnacle of achievement, both for me and for my family. My mother wrote me a letter:

> My dearest Susie. My love I send you, of that you may be sure. But I will tell you also how very happy I am that you have attained a goal that you have been working towards for so long. I am sure there must have been many times when the burden has been very great, and I know only too well that you are now only on the threshold of what I hope will be a long and satisfying career. There is no need to say how full of pride Daddy would have been of all the daughters that he loved so much. Or how Doctor Mac would have said, "I told you so, Susie"! Be happy in your chosen career and know that whatever happens in the future the ties of love that bind us as a family will always be there. My love as always.

I had already decided that, before I took up my first job, I wanted to do something special that I would never forget. I had been saving money from my grant (those really were the halcyon student days) while revising for finals, and I decided to spend it on a trip to America. I had a friend who lived in Washington. I spent six weeks on the east coast of America, on a Greyhound bus, going from Washington to Boston to Florida to Atlanta, visiting all the places I had heard of but knew nothing about. I had no idea what to expect from each place, but I was open to the new experience and made friends along the way. Sometimes, when I tired of explaining to new acquaintances that I had just qualified as a doctor and dealing with the questions that always seemed to follow, I would pretend to be Judy instead. It was a funny way of getting inside my sister's skin, and of course not difficult for me. I was twenty-eight and we had spent our entire lives knowing the minute details of what the other was doing. It was silly, and after a while I went back to being me. I was a newly qualified doctor, and I submitted again to their questions about what kind of doctor I would be. "Just an ordinary doctor," I replied. "Just the ordinary kind."

My first job as a trainee GP found me at a practice in Highbury. This was handy in terms of geography, but the reality of a GP's life came as something of a shock. As a GP trainee I had very little contact with my trainer. I simply saw one patient after another and did not feel part of a team. It felt quite isolating. After years spent working in a busy hospital, with close colleagues, I quickly discovered that this quiet life did not entirely suit me. In between my morning surgery and my evening surgery I would arrange to meet friends. Soon I was looking forward to the lunches more than to the surgeries, and I realised that I needed to think a little laterally. Being a GP was all very well, it was a useful and necessary job, but if I were going to do it for forty years, I needed to do something else as well. As I cast about for what that something else might be, a friend suggested to me over supper one evening that she had heard that P&O were looking for a ship's doctor to work on their cruise ships. It sounded like just the kind of side dish of excitement my life required.

I sent in an application and was duly called in for interview. Shortly afterwards a letter arrived, telling me they would offer me a position when one became available. Positions were not permanent but were offered on a cruise-by-cruise basis. I tucked away the knowledge that, while there was no opening now, I was at least in the P&O system, and I got on with my day job, occasionally pausing to wonder if or when I would receive a call.

I finished my first six months of GP training and had heard nothing from them. I was just about to move for the second six-month job at a surgery in Chingford when, finally, P&O called. A vacancy had come up and they wondered if I wanted to fill it. This meant flying to Australia to join the SS *Oriana* in Sydney. It sounded hugely exciting, and I had no hesitation in accepting. The elderly doctor, Dr Helen Wagstaff, who was the partner at the second GP practice where I was due to start, proved incredibly understanding. In her day she had travelled a great deal and she agreed that I couldn't possibly pass up such an adventure. Within ten days I was packed up. I acquired the essentials of the uniform and had been given some epaulettes and other items of uniform that P&O specified by a Naval outfitter, although some of the details of what I required remained a touch vague. Hoping I had everything needed, I flew to Bahrain, where my sister Judy was working as a teacher, and spent a few days with her and her husband, before flying on to Sydney. I spent a day in Sydney, as a tourist, and then I embarked on *Oriana* and what was to be a very steep seafaring learning curve.

Oriana was the last of the Orient Steam Navigation Company's ocean liners, launched in 1959, and took up to 2,000 passengers. I was not the only doctor on board, rather my position was that of assistant surgeon, under Dr Peter Mayner, a seasoned P&O senior doctor. There were also two nurses. Even with the four of us it was still a busy time on board. My brief was to look after the ship's crew, while Peter looked after the passengers. But the work was shared to an extent. Crew Surgery took place every morning at 7.30am and at 4.30pm. After morning surgery I would have breakfast with the medical team, and then help Peter deal with any passengers who needed attention. They were treated as private patients and had to claim the cost from their travel insurance. Ailments ranged from sea sickness to heart attacks. Much was chronic disease management, as in land-based general practice. Occasionally there were deaths at sea. While this was obviously sad, it was not that infrequent given the relatively elderly nature of many of the passengers. Our resources were limited to simple blood tests and X-rays, and there was a small operating theatre for minor procedures. If someone had something too serious for us to deal with, Peter would arrange medical care for them in the next port we reached, and we would disembark them on arrival. I learned a great deal from Peter. With his years of experience and my newly qualified ideas, we could manage most things.

A couple of medical presentations remain in my mind from that first cruise. One passenger had had her first ever romance while on board. This had led her to lose her virginity, which she had kept for forty-one years. She had a badly torn vagina which needed several stitches. She insisted that the sex was consensual, but now, with the benefit of my forensic experience, I think that was unlikely. Rape doesn't necessarily produce any injury, but consensual sex rarely does. Looking back, if I had interviewed her more skilfully she might have given a different account. I did ask her what had happened, but as I now know women don't always feel able to say. If she had made an allegation, I wonder how it would have been tackled within the microcosm of the ship. Obviously a set of procedures existed for dealing with criminal incidents. But in that case I never found out, as my patient had decided that there was nothing to report.

Later in the cruise, we were confronted with an outbreak of herpes. I knew quite a lot about the theory of the disease, but I had little clinical experience of it. It is relatively easy to diagnose, presenting as chicken-pox-like blisters on the genitals. Some patients were very ill and one had to be admitted to the hospital for nursing care. At some point during the treatment of this outbreak, it dawned on me that my assumption that passengers and crew did not have sex with each other was clearly misplaced. Had I been a researcher or an epidemiologist I could have produced a fascinating treatise on the incubation and infectiousness of herpes. I quickly came to think that, judging by the presentation of passengers, the incubation period was much less than the medical books of the time suggested. But I was an ordinary doctor, not an academic or a researcher, and I had my hands full dealing with the practical challenge of treating the outbreak.

Thus, it is fair to say that while being a ship's doctor sounded glamorous, in medical terms it was not. But that did not matter to me – all medical experience was good experience at that point, and this was an interesting way to get it. I learned a great deal from Peter, both medically and in terms of my career aspiration. Memorably, somewhere along that first cruise, he told me that a ship's doctor was not a proper medical career, and I shouldn't get so carried away with working for P&O that I neglected to build my career on more solid ground. Given that he had spent his working life as a ship's doctor, this advice initially bounced off me. I was heady with the new experiences I was living on a daily basis, and I paid little attention to his words. I was enjoying it all, as we sailed along the Australian coast and then to Fiji and Tonga, and back again. The port visits were stunning and the people were interesting and I was loving the adventure. But months later I would remember Peter's words, and they would be the prompt needed to finish my training as a GP. But at this point the opportunity to visit places new to me, and to try new things, was overwhelmingly wonderful.

The cruise took in several legs around Australasia, before heading back to Sydney, collecting more passengers and heading in the direction of home. I particularly remember our stop at New Caledonia and going snorkelling for the first time. I went to places I had never been to and had never expected to go to. We stopped in Hong Kong for three days so that passengers could go on trips to China. I had to stay within radio contact of the ship to provide medical cover, as Peter was accompanying passengers on the visit to China. But even three days in the Ocean Terminal in Hong Kong with my walkie-talkie felt important. It was remarkable that I was even there. I was seeing the world and living quite a different life to that of a trainee GP feeling isolated and overwhelmed back in Chingford.

While it was my first cruise, for many of the passengers cruising was a passion and this was just the latest in a long line of trips. As the new girl, I had some catching up to do in terms of learning about the cruise ship way of life. I had to get to grips with the language: to refer to the bow, not the front of the ship, and the deckhead not the ceiling. I also had to understand the routines of life on a ship. A cruise ship is like a self-sufficient little town, with lots of particular ways of doing things. Thankfully colleagues were helpful, as I had no induction period or training. I had to learn on the job, but I soon got into the rhythm.

And there was a rhythm. Cruise ships operate on a regular schedule of activities and meals and, as a doctor, I was expected to dine with guests. I was allocated a table of passengers to sit and eat with each night, and over each leg of the cruise got to know my new clutch of passengers. They loved to talk about other cruises they had taken, and about how this one compared. I could see why for some older people cruising had become the holiday of choice

– the travel was easy, safe and everything was laid on, with minimal packing and unpacking and general disruption. Many of them didn't even get off the ship when it docked at its various ports of call. It was a self-contained world from which they could look out and view new things, a bit like travelling through a country without ever getting off the coach. There were very few real travellers on board and hardly any contact with the outside world. The ship produced a daily newspaper which was posted under every cabin door, and this noted any big news happening in the UK. Then it moved on swiftly to listing the day's activities, such as Bridge at 10am and aerobics at 11am, followed by drinks with the Deputy Captain at midday. We really were very cut off. One of the biggest risks the passengers faced, it seemed to me, was overeating and overdrinking – there was a great deal of alcohol consumed – as no one was thinking about driving home, and we would sit down to three-course meals every night. Food and its enjoyment played a big part on the cruise, and it was at this point in my life I decided always to decline dessert!

After dinner each night there was entertainment of a very high standard. Even getting to know the entertainers was fascinating. A whole group of people who I would never have met in my previous life.

I wore a uniform every day, something I had not done since my years at the Red Cross and school, which felt quite strange at first. I minded this small loss of self-determination at first, and in the early days of my seafaring adventures I would quietly try to customise my uniform.

One evening I remember I wore a pink tie round my neck, to give me a little individuality. I even danced with the Captain of the ship that night, which felt very special as I was such a junior officer and the Captain is an important figure on any ship. Peter didn't say a word at the time, but ticked me off later. He knew I was rebelling against the system a little. Ultimately the rules were that if I was on duty then I was in uniform. If I wasn't on duty but wanted to go into the public rooms, I had to be in uniform. But essentially I was *always* on duty. I gradually came to accept it. I understood the thinking behind the discipline – it was designed to show that I was an officer. P&O had neglected to tell me to purchase a hat, and I spent my entire first cruise borrowing one from someone or other as I could, or alternatively apologising for not having one. The evening wear was a white shirt and a long black skirt. The shirt was made of polyester and when we stopped in Hong Kong, which was well known for its rapid tailoring services, I had mine copied in pure silk, which felt much nicer to wear. It was not an exciting evening outfit, but I came to understand that it was necessary.

I also struggled with being on call all the time. I was always on call overnight, and I had to wear the uniform for every call I made. The only time I wore my own clothes was when I went on shore leave. Peter Mayner was very good about making sure I could go ashore. He had been with P&O for twenty years or more and had been to every port we called at many times. He didn't need to do it again and, very fairly, he let me go if he could. He also took responsibility for landing sick patients if we were disembarking them en route to hospital.

I remember one horrendous incident, which did result in the landing of a patient. We were nearing Papua New Guinea when I was called to see a patient who had fallen down a very steep set of steps and split her scalp open very badly. She was taken to the ship's hospital and I started sewing her up. She was awake, and as we were talking she was telling me about how she fell; it then occurred to me that she might have broken her neck. There was so much blood I had been focusing on that, but now I paused in my sewing for a moment to ask the assistant if we had some sandbags with which to stabilise the neck. Fortunately we did. After we put them in place, I finished stitching up her scalp and then we did some X-rays. From these it was immediately obvious that she had dislocated her neck and her spine was out of line. I told Peter, who agreed that we could not deal with this on board. She was either going to need surgery or she would need external fixation to stay very still while it repaired itself. She had had a near miss, because if the spinal cord had been impinged, she might have been paralysed.

As soon as possible, Peter took responsibility for organising a hospital place. When a patient needed to be landed, the process of how and where this was done had to be meticulously thought through in advance. In this instance, landing the patient was not straightforward. She had to be placed in a Neil Robertson Stretcher, which is similar to a straitjacket for the entire body. As we were unable to moor in the port, we had to put her over the side of the ship into a small boat, and from there take her to hospital. Once admitted, she had to stay in hospital for six weeks, but happily her neck was externally fixed without surgery. That incident was a great lesson to me, as it taught me not to look just at the blood. It is the same principle that applies at the scene of an accident: don't rush to attend to the person who is shouting the loudest, as there is clearly nothing wrong with their airway! Ever since, when I am on board ship, or going down steep stairs, I always put a hand on the rail.

Deciding to put a person ashore was a particular kind of challenge. Once they had been landed, it was very unlikely the ship would be able to come back for them. There is a whole industry built on international medical transfers. A ship has an agent in every port, which makes it a bit easier.

When a passenger died on-board, we would issue the death certificate and the body, and the family member or friend they were travelling with, would be disembarked at the next stop, and flown directly home. The ship had a morgue, but those travelling with the deceased understandably never wanted to finish the cruise in such circumstances.

My own adventure came to an abrupt and premature end in a totally unexpected way: I fell ill myself as we were coming through the Panama Canal. I remember feeling terrible about this for Peter. Generally, when someone on board was unwell, we could discuss it together. This time the patient was me, and he couldn't discuss it with anyone. I had some kind of fever that came on very fast, and Peter's concern was that I had meningitis. He landed me in Florida and I went into hospital there, where I stayed for a few days before being flown home to the UK and admitted to Barts Hospital. Slowly I recovered from the mystery illness. I had never been seriously ill before, and it served as a lesson to me of what life is like on the patient's side of things. I hated having to explain to doctors what the matter was. I was always as concise as possible when it came to giving doctors a history, as I had by that point experienced countless rambling patients who started their story, "Well, doctor, the pain began three weeks ago last Thursday and I'd just eaten a banana…" or something similar. I don't remember all the details of the illness, but I must have been significantly unwell for Peter to be so worried that I needed to be landed. I understood his decision, as he had all the crew and passengers to consider. When I recovered I felt terribly embarrassed, and was worried that P&O would no longer employ me as a result. There was no way of knowing except to wait and see if they called again.

I took up my second six months of GP training in East London with Dr Wagstaff and concentrated on the job I did have. Dr Wagstaff showed me a different style of general practice. She ran the practice from her front room, breaking for coffee at eleven, when we would discuss patients and generally collaborate. It felt a much less isolating experience than my previous GP training post, and I focused on how much I was learning and how close I was getting to qualification in general practice. However, in early summer, P&O contacted me again. They told me they wanted to have me back and I was thrilled. Once again, I was invited onto the *Oriana*, this time to go on a cruise in the Mediterranean.

A little wiser this time, I purchased my own hat before I left. There was a different senior surgeon on this trip, but the set-up was similar to the previous cruise. Again, I enjoyed the travel aspect, and the challenges presented by life on board. Simple things like passengers who would come on board and not bring the medication they needed, in the naïve belief that we would carry every possible medicine. I would have to spend hours poring over the *British National Formulary* working out which drugs were safe to use instead. Simple requests ashore can be solved by a quick call to the local pharmacy. However, at sea there is no local pharmacist to ask and no wholesaler to deliver by the evening. But at the back of my mind Peter Mayner's words were niggling at me. Much as I enjoyed being at sea, I knew I also needed to build a proper medical career, so I continued to balance the demands of P&O with finishing my GP training. By the autumn of 1981, I was back working with Dr Wagstaff, who remained remarkably amenable to my stop-start GP training style and allowed me to accommodate my itchy feet. At Christmas I went on a cruise as the ship's doctor on SS *Uganda*, taking my mother with me. She was very proud to be the mother of the ship's doctor, the only time she ever saw me at work.

In January 1982, a cold bleak month at the best of times in the UK, with just weeks until my GP qualification was complete, another call came, with an offer to join a world cruise on SS *Canberra*. The cruise was leaving from Southampton and would take three months. It was calling at lots of exciting-sounding places. Sunshine and adventure were yet again on my horizon. The pay as a ship's doctor was less than I earned as a trainee GP, but of course all my living costs were covered. It felt absolutely impossible to pass up. Within a few days, my bags were packed, Dr Wagstaff was waving me off yet again, and once more I was setting off to sea.

Canberra had been launched in 1961, particularly to run between the UK and Australia when emigration was popular. She was P&O's most expensive ship to date and could take over 2,000 passengers. However, as airfares fell in the 1960s, she was refitted and repurposed, becoming a very successful cruise ship. Everyone on *Oriana* had told me that *Canberra* was a fantastic ship to work on. I couldn't wait to find out.

The cruise lasted three months. Life on a ship is very much its own world and, absorbed as I was by the challenges of each day, there was little time to take much interest in the outside world. People rarely talked about politics or what was going on at home. It was easy to disengage with shore life, and to exist on a day-to-day basis. By the end of March 1982 we were on the final leg of the world cruise, and thoughts were turning to arriving home, when I first heard the news of an Argentinian invasion of British territory. Everyone on board started wondering where the Falklands actually were. Some people thought they were just a little further away than the Shetlands. While we grappled with geography, the news of the invasion and crisis certainly did not feel as if it had anything to do with us.

How wrong we were. We had just left Naples and were heading towards Gibraltar when we heard the next bulletin: Mrs Thatcher had decided to assemble a task force to retake the islands. Potentially, seemingly almost overnight, the UK was going to be involved in a war.

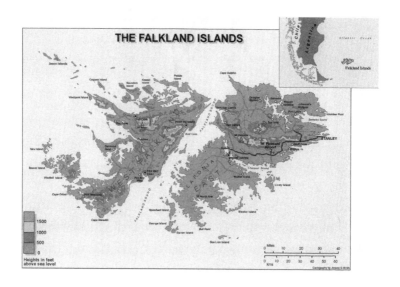

THE FALKLAND ISLANDS

FIVE

Suddenly the ship was buzzing. No longer was the dinner menu the main topic of conversation. I started tuning into the World Service in my cabin, and on deck, rumours started to do the rounds. Passengers and crew swapped stories of what they had heard and the feeling grew that this Falklands situation could be a big issue. Margaret Thatcher was clearly not taking the invasion lying down, the government were scrambling about trying to get organised after having been caught on the back foot, and a task force had to be put together and dispatched to reclaim the islands as soon as possible.

Meanwhile, I was learning new facts at breakneck speed. The Falkland Islands were nowhere near the Shetlands but were actually 8,000 miles away from the UK, just three hundred miles from the coast of South America. They were a long way from home, and there wasn't any obvious nearby base for the British forces to set up camp to defend the islands. Significant Naval support was going to be required as part of any task force.

We were sailing towards the Straits of Gibraltar when we learned of an unscheduled pause in our progress. At that point we all knew something serious was afoot. A basic rule of a large ship is that a small boat would never approach when the ship is underway. Any arrangements to visit a port are always made well in advance, and that is when stores and any new passengers are collected. But now Captain Scott-Masson had authorised a rendezvous with a small craft containing a number of mysterious people. These people turned out to be a reconnaissance party from the British Government, who had come to assess the *Canberra* and work out whether she had potential to assist in the operation. A crew member more experienced in the ways of Naval warfare explained to me about the practice of requisitioning merchant ships at times when the Royal Navy did not have enough ships. The process of Ships Taken Up From Trade (STUFT) had previously happened in wartime to support the Navy. It seemed that *Canberra* was now being considered as a part of the task force.

Soon a new rumour began to circulate. Apparently one of the personnel picked up off Gibraltar was a doctor, and he wanted to assess the medical department of the ship. This turned out to be correct, and the individual in question was Surgeon Commander Rick Jolly. As it became apparent that there was a considerable chance *Canberra* would be going to war, I told him that I would be happy to be part of any medical team. A doctor would still be required to look after the crew; I was willing and available and also accustomed to the ship. Looking back, I had no understanding of what I was volunteering for but at the time I had no doubts at all. It simply seemed the sensible thing to do. I was not the only one volunteering. Angela, a nurse who had also been on the world cruise, was determined to go. I liked Angela, we worked well together, and it felt reassuring that, if we went, we would be going together.

Rick Jolly didn't turn me down, but he did point out that, in the Navy, women did not go to sea. (Although this is no longer the case. Women became eligible to go to sea in the Navy in 1990.) However, I reminded him that I wasn't in the Navy, and that doctors would clearly be required. He told me he would see what he could do.

It took three days to sail from Gibraltar to Southampton, and all the talk was no longer about the new passengers due to embark, but about what might happen next. We didn't have to wait long for answers. As soon as we docked, the passengers were disembarked. The next cruise that had been planned had been cancelled, and a team of engineers came aboard to start to refit *Canberra* as a multi-purpose military ship. No longer were we cut off from the outside world, shielded from news. Headlines on newspapers and television channels soon made it apparent there was a national feeling afoot that the Falklands should be reclaimed. A fleet of warships and support vessels was being prepared, and *Canberra* was to be a support ship. She would help transfer troops and act as a hospital ship.

Changes had to be made to *Canberra* as quickly as

possible. Things that would have taken months took a couple of days. Swimming pools were drained and one was covered over to become a flight deck; another flight deck was constructed on the sunbathing area. The sleeping capacity of 1,500 passengers was reorganised to take up to 3,000 troops. The work continued through the night, such was the sense of urgency.

Meanwhile, I remained on board and waited to find out if I would be taken up on my offer to go. A day later, without any reason being given, I was told that I was authorised to sail south with the *Canberra*. So, too, could Angela. Rick Jolly later told me he had argued the case for us. Similarly, the Chief Officer of *Canberra*, Martin Reed, had also apparently put our case forward. However it had come about, I was grateful that it had. The end result was I was now part of the team going to the Falklands, and soon. A large military medical team was being assembled, and I soon happily discovered we were to work under the guidance of my old acquaintance Dr Peter Mayner. I'd worked well with him before, liked him, and was delighted that he was going to be heading up our team.

Now I knew I was going, the frenzied activity going on around swept outwards to include us in the medical department. We would be setting off soon, although I didn't know yet precisely when, and there was a lot to do. There was absolutely no time to stand still. Within a few hours, instructions came from the Ministry of Defence that we needed to sign the Official Secrets Act. This was followed shortly afterwards by a request from P&O head office that we all had to make our wills, and lodge them in their office forthwith. This last was a sobering request. I was only thirty-one and it had never crossed my mind that I ought to have written a will. Now, of course, it made sense so I did as requested. It was strange to be confronted with the prospect of my own death. I got on with packing up all the souvenirs I had bought on the various stops around the world, to send home to my sisters. With the writing of my will in my mind, I remember packing in a swirl of mixed feelings. I had bought a gorgeous pair of leather boots in Naples, and as I put them into the suitcase I thought they would really suit Judy if I didn't make it back.

My mother came to Southampton to collect the suitcase, as I wasn't allowed to leave the ship. Married officers were allowed to have their spouse on board overnight and I felt it was unfair that my mother wasn't allowed to even visit me on board. I spoke to a senior officer and shortly afterwards an exception was made. I was very glad to spend a little time with her before I went. She was clearly not happy that I had committed to go to the Falklands, but at the time it didn't really occur to me why, beyond the fact that she might worry about me. Now, again with hindsight, I have a better understanding of what she must have been feeling. My mother had been a young woman during the Second World War and knew first-hand what the reality of war looked like. She may never have spoken of it, but she knew precisely what war meant, in a way that I didn't yet understand. She knew about losing people she loved to bombing raids; she knew about the wholesale damage war could do to families and to property. She knew all about living in fear on a daily basis. Now one of her daughters was choosing to sail off into this kind of dangerous unknown. But there was nothing she could do but accept it. It was too late to change my mind, and anyway I didn't want to. Even though I had had to write a will, even though I had left most of my possessions to my family, I still didn't really think that anything would happen to me. We were a support ship, not a military ship and I was there to help in a medical capacity, not to fight. I hugged my mother goodbye and told her not to worry. She said "Susie, if I were in your position I would do exactly the same. Off you go my love, I'm proud of you."

The ship started to load. Some 3,000 troops came on board carrying their packs. We were taking the Royal Marines and 3 Parachute regiment. As they settled in, the loading continued. Vast quantities of provisions were required to feed everyone on board, as on this mission there would be no real prospect of being able to stop in ports to replenish supplies. Military equipment piled up on the deck. More people arrived: some seventeen Naval doctors, a Naval entourage to augment the P&O crew, together with a press corps of about ten.

The urgency produced results. On the evening of Friday 9 April, astonishingly just a mere fifty-six hours after we had ended the world cruise, SS *Canberra* slipped her ropes and pulled out of Southampton harbour. The atmosphere was electric. I was one of just fifteen women on board. We lined the ship's side as we sailed off and waved to the many well-wishers on the dockside. A regimental band played

'Land of Hope and Glory' on the dockside, while relatives and friends waved back. While it was an extraordinary send-off, it was not a holiday that we were going on, but to a possible conflict zone.

Captain Scott-Masson, who had worked for P&O since 1950, and captained of *Canberra* on the world cruise that we had just completed, had, like many of P&O's *Canberra* ship's company, elected to stay with the ship come what may. He sounded the horn as we left Southampton behind, and slowly, as England faded from view, we all drifted away from the railings and went to do whatever we thought we should do next, settling into the first moments of a new reality.

Canberra sets sail for the South Atlantic.

SIX

As the heady moments of departure died away, a feeling of anti-climax descended on the ship. The Navy had allocated a Senior Naval Officer, Captain Christopher Burne, to work with Captain Scott-Masson. Despite the addition of Captain Burne, Captain Scott-Masson was still very much in charge. All the preparations that had made us fit for war were in evidence. The ship was carrying troops rather than a host of passengers keen to see something of the world, but still there was a strong feeling that we might be turned back at any moment. We all half-expected the news to come at any time that the Argentinians had surrendered, and the conflict was already over. Some people joked we'd be sailing for home again before we reached the Isle of Wight. I suppose, with hindsight, these kinds of remarks had something of the over-optimistic flavour of "the war will be over by Christmas," which had been the British attitude at the opening of the First World War. That prediction had been proved very wrong, and so it was with this one.

The Isle of Wight came and went, and we continued to make our way towards the South Atlantic.

The further we got from home, the more a sense of tension began to gather. Daily events reminded us that we were heading to a war zone. I ran a morning surgery each day for the crew, and every now and then someone mentioned feeling nervous about where we were heading. The troops trained every day on deck, thundering around in their boots with their packs on their backs.

The crew and the troops inevitably mixed, and there was a quiet respect between us, all of us there to perform our different roles. I was there as a medic, to look after the crew but also the troops if it became necessary, a thought which at this point I still kept filed away in the back of my mind. I remember some of the young Naval pilots, just twenty or twenty-one, expressing their amazement that they were going to war at all.

"I joined the Navy to fly helicopters," one young man said to me with a look of astonishment on his face. Now these lads were facing a very different reality. It made me pause and consider what made a young person join the forces. Sometimes their stories fitted the model of a young man leaving school with no clear direction ahead, and who then found the focus needed to grow up fully through a stint in the armed forces, with all the opportunities that offered. Whether these young men had ever really expected to go to war was another matter. But there is nothing like a conflict to make a person understand the point of the armed forces.

Although there were very few women on the ship, in

terms of my work it didn't matter. No one I treated seemed even to notice that I was a woman. It was as if the uniform rendered my gender irrelevant. I was a doctor and that was all that mattered. Yet the world of 1982 was much less committed to equality between the sexes than it is today, and female officers in the Navy weren't yet allowed to see active service. I mixed with the officers on board, and I ate in the restaurant with the officers and the journalists every day. Robert Fox, John Shirley and Max Hastings were on board, amongst others, covering the conflict for their respective newspapers. Producing quantities of good food was something that P&O excelled at. The food they turned out was impressive, particularly given that the number of covers was double what the galley had been used to producing for civilian trips.

Sometimes I couldn't face the dining room and I would slip down to the galley and collect a few things to eat in my cabin, such as a bread roll and some salad. Everyone needs a quiet night in. The galley crew were always good to me, as I knew them through my work as crew doctor; one of my responsibilities was to inspect the galley regularly for hygiene.

While at the back of my mind I dreaded getting to know someone who would later be killed, it was also hard to stay completely detached from the people all around. Inevitably, I got to know many of the other officers, and gradually built a rapport. It was a necessary way to get through the uncertainty of what lay ahead. We all needed to be able to talk to a few friends in the privacy of our cabins about what might or might not happen. We knew that in theory it was an extreme situation we were facing, but it hadn't yet come into full view, so we didn't know exactly the shape it would take. From our perspective, no shot had been fired, no soldier lost. But the underlying sense of apprehension was growing daily. Company was also a distraction to take our minds away from the possible.

By 20 April, we had reached Ascension Island. Lying just off its coast, we waited to see what we would be told to do next. As the ship's ordinary doctor, I wasn't kept informed of what was planned, or what was going on. Like most of the crew, I was dependent on announcements from the Captain to keep up to date on plans and events, or I had to glean my news from any other source I could. Usually, this latter was word of mouth, from one officer to another, and it couldn't always be relied on. This lack of information in between announcements gave a continual sense of uncertainty. There were many different routes for information to filter down. One of my dear friends was the Radio Officer and he was a wonderful source of information. Much of the time he was not allowed to say what he knew. So we became expert at working out what he was *not* saying to get updated. The Chief Officer Martin Reed was always good to the Medical Department and, supplied with enough tea, he would often let us know if the latest buzz was true or false. We were sailing on the brink of a war but we were not quite in it. Frenzied activity was all around us, but we had no real idea what the plan was. It was disconcerting, but also a lesson in giving up all attempts at self-determination.

We just had to wait until someone saw fit to tell us what would be happening next. Or, if no one did, for events to unfold.

The postal service was hugely important on military ships at that time. Letter writing was what we all fell back on to keep connected with those we had left behind. I wrote to my sisters and my mother almost daily and would wait anxiously for their replies. Letters were collected and dropped off by helicopter several times each day. The act of writing in itself was offering me some kind of comfort. As well as frequent letters home, I took up diary writing again and started scribbling down my thoughts and feelings. Looking back through the letters, which my sisters and mother kept, and the diaries, reminds me of the way a sense of fear crept up. In a letter to Judy, sent on 10 April, when we had just set sail, I was full of jokes:

"We're really quite cheerful. Stickers abound, like 'Maggie chooses P&O cruises.'"

But just two days later, I was striking a different tone. A letter on 12 April, to Penny, notes:

"I'm becoming intermittently scared. I suppose the mode of dying is more frightening than dying itself but finding out we will be a legitimate target when we get down there has not cheered me up. I just pray that our present passengers don't become our patients."

I also wrote to my mother. She was living in my house, and I was glad of it. I wrote to one of my sisters that, if I did not come back, I would like the garden to be kept planted only with yellow flowers, my favourite colour, and eventually, after my mother's death, to be left to Janny's daughter, who was then my only niece. Looking back, it was a rather miserable letter for members of my family to receive, but it shows where my thinking was heading.

Many of my diary entries also reflect my state of mind. Three days after our arrival at Ascension Island we moored close to the island. Troops were put ashore for weapons training but the rest of us were not allowed to disembark. From our position on the water, as we sailed around the island waiting for our next order, we could sometimes watch some of the comings and goings of the military and there was no getting away from facts: this was war.

23 April 1982: Today … this situation became a reality. The operations going on are absolutely breath-taking. Helicopters were queuing up in the air to land on the flight deck. The noise of the activities is exciting but the job is so sinister. They're … transferring ammunition, torpedoes, mortar bombs. If half of what I've heard is true, then we would go up like a glowing mushroom if we got hit. Yesterday, we in the medical department were shown over a lifeboat. It was the afternoon, when the troops were running around the Prom. Deck, pounding away in their green rigs with packs of all sorts of things on their backs, helicopters deafening us every other minute. It made it all seem deadly serious. We were looking at survival rations, not out of interest or novelty, but knowing that our lives might depend on them at any time. It's not a remote possibility, but something to be taken into consideration.

We are constantly trying to analyse our own and other people's motives … for me it's simple … there was no alternative.

The sense that the ship was vulnerable to attack was growing all the time. Cruise ships are traditionally lit up like Christmas trees, and *Canberra* was no exception. Somewhere on the journey to Ascension Island, blackout measures had been introduced. However, blackout was hard to enforce and the ship, gleaming white rather than a military grey, was quickly given the nickname of the Great White Whale. All this added to the feeling that, to the Argentinians, we were a legitimate target – a sitting duck to even the most short-sighted bomber pilot.

We were to spend close to three weeks waiting at Ascension Island, before finally being sent on to the Falklands. In my daily morning surgeries for the crew, when I treated whatever ailments they had, I saw a growing number who voiced concerns that they hadn't really understood what they were getting themselves into. Nerves were jangling, and I totally understood why. A few, who really felt they could go no further, were put off at Ascension Island and returned home. But the rest of us remained on board and continued to wait for the next phase in our part of this conflict.

23 April: Last night things began to happen … I met someone who said that an unidentified submarine had turned up or been detected. I rapidly returned to the cabin and then all the lights went out and we plunged

into total darkness. There was no light even in the night sky. We have a total blackout.

The Falklands War had started when the Argentinians had invaded the capital of the Falkland Islands, Port Stanley, on 2 April. On 3 April, they had also taken South Georgia, a second island in the cluster that makes up the territory. The British destroyer HMS *Antrim* had arrived near South Georgia on 21 April, and on 25 April, after a couple of false starts, retook the territory. This apparently led to celebrations back home, but no real change to our position circling around Ascension Island. We were still no clearer as to when we would move on to the Falklands, which lay about seven days' sailing away.

As we waited for instructions, the ship started to feel claustrophobic. The decks were much less open than before, as containers were lined up on them, and we were carrying more people than the ship had been built for. From my previous trips with P&O I was used to being able to get off at ports and spend some time on shore. Now this was not an option for any of the crew on the ship. We had to find our own way to deal with this enforced incarceration. Sometimes, after a shift, I'd gratefully retreat to the comfort and space of my cabin, which was rather wonderful, with a bunk and a shower and a porthole, a radio and my books and my letters from home. It was just round the corner from the hospital, and while I was never off call for the entire three months we were away, which was a stressful demand in itself, I could snatch some quiet time when I wasn't needed. I could enjoy a private conversation with Angela or another colleague or spend time writing home to my family or in my diary. All of that was necessary downtime, in the face of the uncertainty of what might be coming next.

The next big event came on 2 May, when the news came through on the World Service that a Royal Navy submarine had sunk the *Belgrano*, an Argentinian warship, with over 300 lives lost. This was a hugely sobering moment. The ship fell quiet as everyone took in the implications, the loss of life involved, and the fact that now it seemed utterly unlikely that this conflict was going away. Seafarers were getting killed, and in the medical department we were all very distressed about that. We were there to save lives, but hundreds had now gone beyond any help we could offer. This war – or conflict, as it was officially called, in the absence of war actually being declared – was really happening. We were near to the conflict zone and were biding time until we received orders that would involve going into it.

With the sinking of the *Belgrano*, we felt the unspecified threat to *Canberra* more keenly. Within hours, rumours began that the Argentinians wanted to sink a large ship in return. We were a large ship. We were a large white ship, highly visible on the seas, even at night. It was an uncomfortable thought. The sea looked calm, but underneath, invisible, possibly lurked submarines with the capacity to sink us. After that day, we worried about the underwater threat quietly but continually, never quite certain if it was real or imagined. Men always looked happier when their shifts were served higher up on the ship than deep in the bowels. We all understood without it ever being discussed that, if we were holed, those who were in the depths of *Canberra* were the least likely to survive. We all did our best to avoid actively discussing these fears. Morale had to be kept up, and Captain Scott-Masson and Senior Naval Officer Chris Burne did a good job at this. Captain Scott-Masson was still very much the Captain of the ship as we sailed to war, although he left all things military to Captain Burne. They worked well together. Everything on board was very well managed, and as a member of the crew, rather than the military, I felt that Captain Scott-Masson was speaking to and looking out for me. Scott-Masson, I discovered much later on, was a Naval Reservist, as were many of the other P&O ship's company. Their experience meant they were well adapted to the situation we faced now. He carried off the challenge with an air of calm and confidence that permeated down to us all.

The next day, we heard that the *Queen Elizabeth II* (*QE2*) had been requisitioned from rival shipping company Cunard. On 4 May, an Exocet sank HMS *Sheffield*, a Type 42 destroyer, in what was widely seen as retaliation for the sinking of the *Belgrano*. Some twenty men were killed with another twenty-six injured. This was another terrible loss, but it did little to quell the rumours that the Argentinians were still after something bigger.

The conflict was escalating, losses were mounting, and still we waited. We spent our time preparing for casualties, establishing a blood bank and attending lectures. Early

Peter Mayner and me in the sick bay on *Oriana*.

Below: Hospital dinner party.

Bottom: The galley crew after rounds with the deputy captain.

21 May 1982. Dawn in San Carlos Water.

POWs in the passenger lounge.

Below: Operating on board.

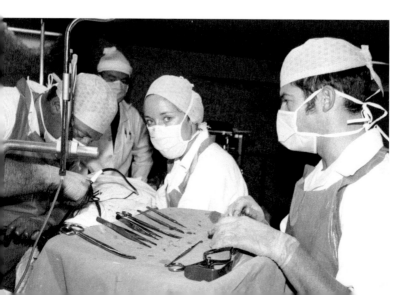

A view of the ward with blacked-out windows and naval staff.

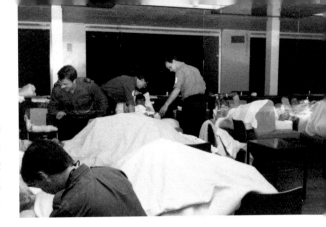

On the bridge approaching South Georgia.

Below: Visit to SS *Uganda* after the surrender.

Port Stanley. I got ashore
for 45 minutes.

Below: Beating retreat
on the way home.

Approaching Southampton.

Opposite: P&O ship's company on the
flight deck.

Twins reunited.

The cabin party.

Twenty-five years later.

Rosie, me and Angela at the 25th anniversary commemoration.

The West family in 1996. From left: Penny, Susie, Mother, Jan and Judy.

Judy (right) and me with our mother in 1990.

On RFA *Argus* in Gibraltar.

The Falklands Memorial near the Tower of London, 2021.

on we had established the *Canberra* Medical Society as a way of sharing knowledge, and this added another layer of structure to our days. All these distractions served to keep us busy as we waited off the coast of Ascension Island, loading and unloading before sailing to deeper and safer waters each night in full blackout.

Finally the order came to proceed south, towards the Falklands. It wasn't a shock as we'd been waiting for this instruction, but it was still a significant moment. At the start of the task force being assembled, *Canberra* was only a support ship. But by now we knew we were transporting our troops all the way, wherever this took us and whatever it meant.

We sailed at night, to reduce the risk of attack, and as part of a group, which gave us some feeling of protection. The Argentinian Air Force was a potential threat to us, as were the submarines we couldn't see. However, our Naval capacity was strong, and we reminded ourselves of that. Following the *Belgrano* sinking, the majority of the Argentinian fleet had remained in port. Still, with *Canberra* gleaming white amid the fleet of grey Naval vessels, we couldn't help but feel our vulnerability as we went about our business. Some people were getting jumpy.

My diary entries reflect this:

15 May: "This is the bridge. Underwater threat. Yellow Alert." This is the second time we have had this alert. Yesterday we were on our way to church but turned back. Today I was just packing my combat jacket. I'm

now meant to walk around with my life jacket on. It took a great deal of wheeling and dealing to acquire all my gear. I've done all right but I loathe the 'I'm all right Jack' attitude. We should all be able to get combat jackets and folding life jackets we can work in. Yesterday when the Yellow Alert was on I decided to paint my nails.

18 May: Today started at 7.30am, the alarm bell was ringing constantly. Red Alert. Meaning attack imminent or occurring. I jumped out of bed and tried not to fumble as I clambered into two pairs of trousers, sweatshirt, two woollies, uniform, woolly-pully tracksuit top and combat jacket and lace up shoes and life jacket. Then pick up hat and torch and go round to the hospital. Adrenalin was pacing steadily round my body. My mouth was dry as parchment. I was at first waiting for the crash, explosion or gush of water. Nothing came, and as soon as I was with Angela and Rosie, I felt more normal. I gulped a cup of tea thinking it would keep me warm in the lifeboat. We were told that the threat was unidentified aircraft 180 miles away, which may sound a long way but not when you're flying at 600 miles plus per hour. Well, the threat ended after about 20 minutes and we all looked at each other in our bizarre rig and had to laugh. Then Angela said she wanted a photo so we ended up having another 'team photo' session. Then we went and had some bacon for breakfast which I'm never usually up in time for.

Action was coming nearer as we sailed further south. There

was a rare moment of excitement when we crossed the line of latitude which meant our pay went up 150 per cent. Everyone knew that the goal was to safely unload the troops we were carrying in a bid to retake the islands.

19 May: Last night I saw lots of activity. I went off to the wardroom to watch a film. For the first time I carried my combat jacket with me and my life jacket. It does certainly feel odd. On my return I saw lots of packing and all the troops were up and the chief came to enlighten me. Overcrowding is now a real problem. It now seems to me that the landing will definitely happen on Thursday night, the 20th, but it will not be presented to the world as a counter invasion or an offensive, and if it can be done bloodlessly, then it can be presented as a mere establishment of British presence. They say the Argies want to politically back down under military pressure. That could still be a possibility … there has been a new MOD radio station set up in Ascension Island to broadcast to Argentina in Spanish … I'll finish for now.

20 May: Well, we've just heard over the Tannoy that the instruction has come from the Commander of the Fleet that tonight we will be landing. The assault is nigh. My feelings are difficult to describe. Excitement obviously, anticipation of something challenging yet terrifying. I have to keep saying to myself that I may not get back alive. We had the first corpse brought in today.

I'm now on watch 4–12, then off overnight, then on at

8. There may well be the first casualties in by then.

I'm now sitting gathered with all the great P&O medical team at General Emergency stations – as a precautionary measure. We have just entered the north end of the Falkland Sound. The ships are going in, bow to stern, i.e. nose to tail, and we are about eighth in line. In half an hour we shall be anchoring. Everything is in silence. The ship is closed off and the atmosphere is a tense calm. I've been trying to read Homer. A translation of course. A. has fallen asleep, having made us all laugh too much as usual.

21 May – 1.10am: We are now anchored just off the Falkland Islands, 8,000 miles from home. The cabin still looks the same, it's slightly chillier than a couple of weeks ago but otherwise there is little to suggest that we are now in a position of war. There is gunfire from a destroyer which is anchored. I can just make out land, when I peer out of the blackout, with all the lights off behind me. It's a lovely starlight night – though possibly not so lovely for our landing troops. But presumably if we are firing, that doesn't matter too much now, the Argies must know we are here. Wouldn't it be lovely if they simply surrendered when they realised how serious we are, but I think that's a vain hope.

I must say I'm not too keen on going to bed at the moment, we've been told to go to bed until 4.45 when we up anchor and move off again … 5.10am. The night is very bright and it's easy to see land about 200 yards away.

The rippling wakes against the side radiate outwards and the shadows play tricks, and for a few moments I thought there were figures swimming splashlessly through the water.

12.45pm: We are now anchored up a deep-water creek, San Carlos Water, with about eight other ships. All morning there have been air raids. I was upstairs on A deck, on watch for minor casualties, but as yet there were none. Yet every time the warning came we had to take cover on the deck as deep as possible in the middle of the ship, with all our worldly goods about us. Sometimes we'd get up and then straight away be told to take cover again. It must have happened at least eight times.

21 May was to prove a turning point in the Falklands conflict. It was one of those endless days when we felt the passing of every minute. In a war zone, the tick of the seconds is almost audible. At 5.30am, we entered San Carlos Water, which became known as Bomb Alley. We were still with other ships that were offering us some protection, including HMS *Antrim* and HMS *Plymouth*, HMS *Brilliant* and HMS *Ardent*. We were a team and that offered some comfort. But the Argentinian Air Force were overhead, and many times rockets narrowly missed *Canberra*. At 10am, we began to disembark troops, starting with 42 Commando and then 3 Commando Brigade.

Even from the distance of many years, I remember being struck by the bravery of all those we had transported from

Southampton to the war zone, the troops we had tried not to get too close to, just in case. I watched them disembark, some of them clearly still teenagers, not even in their twenties. The youngest looked like schoolboys. Laden with their packs, their helmets on, some of them still had spots, others barely needed to shave. Many others were older. But active conflict is at least in part a young person's game, and many still bore the gangly frame of a body not yet fully grown. What has stayed with me down the years is the overriding sense of focus, teamwork and cheerfulness they all displayed. The commitment to the cause they had signed up for was astounding, and they were more than ready to get on with it. It is something I still recall every Remembrance Sunday. Watching them go, I simply hoped and prayed that their youthful optimism would not be snuffed out before the day was over. Back home, parents and girlfriends and siblings would be worrying about them. They had done the training, they wore the uniform, but were they aware of what they were going to face? Could anyone ever really be prepared for war, to kill and to die, and to watch colleagues you have trained with and drunk in the pub with be shot or killed?

After the conflict was over, and we were on the way home, this was a question I would raise again with the ship's psychiatrist, Morgan O'Connell. But now wasn't the time for that. Now was about keeping alert, minute after minute, of staying focused and staying alive. Now was Operation Sutton and D-Day.

The Argentinian Air Force started their attack, with wave

after wave of attacking aircraft flying at our flotilla. Much later, after the conflict was over, the Argentinians would claim they had been told to avoid *Canberra*, as they knew it was not a military ship but a support vessel. It certainly didn't feel like that at the time. Many times, rockets narrowly missed us and the order came to take cover. Other military ships were clearly targeted. HMS *Ardent* was hit repeatedly by three waves of enemy aircraft, with bombs and rocket fire. Within hours *Ardent* was very seriously damaged and on fire. When it became clear that she was likely to sink, the order was given to abandon ship. There were rumours of casualties, and survivors were rescued by HMS *Yarmouth* and some were brought to *Canberra*. Enemy aircraft continued to fly over us, and every time I braced, expecting a direct hit. Shortly afterwards, it was decided it was too dangerous for us to remain. The order came through to disembark the rest of the troops on *Canberra*, and as many stores as possible, and for us to leave San Carlos Water for the relative safety of Falkland Sound. Hours of frenzied packing of stores followed, together with further disembarking of troops. Many of the embarked military doctors were also put ashore to establish a field hospital. By 11.15pm, the Great White Whale was withdrawing from 'Bomb Alley', the still burning *Ardent* fading gradually from view.

My diary entry for the next day captured a little of the urgency of that day with immediate hindsight:

22 May: My previous paragraph now reads like the biggest

understatement of all time. The afternoon got hairier than ever and only then did I realise the grave peril we were in and yet survived. People were trying to tell me that they were aiming at other ships but it wasn't true. There were said to be seventeen strikes against us and seven rocket attacks.

In the afternoon we took the casualties and the survivors from the *Ardent* and that was an experience too hard to write about yet. At 4.15 about fifteen casualties arrived together, which doesn't sound many but you think of that number arriving together in an ordinary casualty department. There were so many near misses and merciful escapes, too many to mention.

A great deal had happened in a short time. But there was no time to pause and absorb it. There were no holidays or sick days with this job. Every day, every hour, was one you were on call for. The rigid military structure and the unquestioning following of orders is what enables that to occur, however the day unfolded. Once we were anchored in relative safety, the focus turned to organising the new arrivals, dealing with their injuries, and addressing the bigger picture: how many lives had been lost? Was the conflict turning in our favour?

Soon enough we found out that twenty-two people had been lost in the sinking of the *Ardent*. There was an uplifting moment when the ship's doctor, last seen in the water and presumed lost, turned up amongst the survivors with barely a scratch. But the reality of the cost of war was only too evident now. Most of the survivors we had taken on from the *Ardent* had lost everything they had bar the clothes they stood up in. There were bodies to be buried, and patients to tend to.

By the end of 22 May, survivors had been settled, four of our military had been buried at sea and the Royal Marines band had given a concert to our newly boarded patients. I didn't go to the burials; I'm not sure why, but at the time I think I felt I didn't belong there as I wasn't a serving officer. Now, I see that in fact I essentially *was* serving. I had risked my life in Operation Sutton. But I certainly didn't need to go to the burials to feel the solemnity of what had occurred. Everyone on board felt that, both the military personnel and all the P&O crew. In a short period of time, men had been lost, others remained unaccounted for, ships had been sunk and helicopters downed. Yet the news filtered back to us that it was considered to have gone well for the British. Certainly *Canberra* had done what it had set out to do: it had managed to land all our troops without a single casualty. But still, it was far from over.

23 May: This afternoon I spent in theatre doing debridement of shrapnel wounds with one of the Naval surgeons, which was actually very interesting, not too grisly, well not for me anyway. Sounds awful to say but I thoroughly enjoyed myself.

With casualties on board to tend to, days became busier. The senior surgeons took on the patients with the worst injuries, and I started to attend to those who had been less severely wounded. These men all needed treatment of some kind, but it could vary widely as to what treatment that was. Often I was digging out pieces of shrapnel and stitching up wounds. But a few cases still stand out distinctly in my mind. I remember treating one young man, who had a hole in the skin just under his chin, where a bullet had gone through the soft tissue. It had missed his jaw and tongue by about 1cm, and his jugular vein by 3cm. It was astonishing to realise what a near miss he had had.

Another young man, a helicopter navigator, asked to see me, as he had an injury on his face. I went to see him, and saw he had a cut on his nose and a bruise on one cheek. I examined him and asked him what had happened. The story that he told me revealed that his real wound was an emotional one. The helicopter he had been navigating had been shot down and ditched in the sea. He had managed to release himself, and to get the pilot out as well. He dragged him onto the beach, but the pilot had died in his arms. He had done his best; there was nothing else he could have done. Recounting this to me, he was clearly traumatised and had needed to tell his story. As a doctor on *Canberra*, I was a safe choice. We were all literally in the same boat. He didn't have to bottle up his feelings, and I was very glad that he didn't. I spent about forty-five minutes with him, talking through how he felt now, and how he thought he might feel in the future. This reminder of how important it is to approach patients with sensitivity was something I was to take forward in my career as a GP. Sometimes, my job was first to sit down and listen. Fixing the body from a few scratches is easier than healing the mind of a young person who has witnessed terrible things.

Meanwhile, the conflict raged on. HMS *Antelope* was lost and more casualties were flown on board. The Captain of the *Ardent*, Commander West (no relation) who later became the First Sea Lord, was very visible on board, checking on the well-being of his crew. They might have lost their ship, but they very much remained a unit, led by their Captain.

We were all still trying to find ways to get through the stresses, and one of the ways that I found when I wasn't working was to team up with a few others, usually Angela and Rosie, and pretend we were somewhere else. We developed a variety of tricks. We would have a dinner party in our cabin, and pretend we'd gone out to a local café. Alternatively, we would go to a lecture to distract ourselves, or we would write reports or stocktake to keep busy.

But most of the time it was impossible to get away from what was going on. We were there to mop up the blood, as and when it was spilt. SS *Uganda* had become the principal hospital ship but we were still taking on casualties needing attention.

Early on, we had been told to prepare for the command to abandon ship. Sailing closer to Bomb Alley, that had felt a very likely scenario. Many hours were spent with Angela and Rosie discussing what we would pack if we were told the ship was going down. At first, we all kept a small bag at the ready, packed with essentials, to take to the lifeboat with us if the call came. But as we became more immersed in the war, and more aware of the chaos of destruction, we all came to realise that if the ship was going down, there wouldn't be time to get a bag. There would be no bag. There would be what we stood up in, and what was in our pockets. The three of us agreed that this was reduced to a torch, a picture of family, and a lip salve.

It wasn't the cheeriest of conversations, but it summed up the threat we all lived with, hour by hour, during the conflict. Many times, through the not knowing, the waiting, the blackouts, the false alarms, the sea burials, I was so grateful for the company of Rosie and Angela. Angela was a few years older than me, and she felt more grown up than the rest of us. She was a career P&O nurse and had much more experience than I did. She also had a real gift for humour and would often defuse the tension with jokes, so we would end up in fits of laughter even though we might still be terrified. Rosie was a single woman like me, with a quiet strength. She was senior to Angela, but they felt equal in terms of professional experience. Rosie, also an experienced P&O nurse, had been due to join the ship for the cancelled cruise, and volunteered to come to the Falklands instead.

Through their friendship, I came to understand the essential nature of camaraderie in a war zone; of how relationships were formed and cemented for the period of the war, because of the extraordinary life and death circumstances. On paper, the three of us didn't have much in common, other than our shared professional interest in medicine. But for that life-changing voyage, we were each other's support and companion. The three of us were bonded by the time we spent together, by our commitment to our patients and by the fact we were three of the very small number of women on board, most of whom we never came across. While we mixed amongst the crew and the troops, at every meal, on every walk around the deck, it was just different with Rosie and Angela. We looked out for each other; we were in it together. We could laugh or cry together, and never feel judged and that was a very important release from the stress of life lived at war. Looking back, we had far too much time over the weeks of the conflict to think about what we would do if the ship was hit. We agreed the worst of it would be to be below deck in the event of a strike by an Exocet missile. We also agreed that if we were tending to patients, we would not have been able to leave them. That would have been out of the question.

24 May: We went to the Cricketer's Bar this evening. There was no beer but apart from that there was some semblance of normality. The *Ardent* survivors are conspicuous, partly because they are new faces and partly because some of them have no clothes other than boiler suits, just issued from "slops". Obviously boiler suits are not normally worn in the officers' mess. The whole of our ship simply aches with sympathy for HMS *Ardent*. They can't believe their ship is gone. They are fantastically grateful to us and appreciative of all we do for them.

On 24 May there were several false reports that the *Canberra* had been hit and gone up in flames. Some of these reports went as far as the BBC. Captain Scott-Masson kept a journal through the conflict, later published in part by P&O. On this particular day, he wrote: "Two or three times today it has been reported on the BBC that we have been hit and are sinking – claims by Argentina. I worry for the awful tension this must bring on our ship's company's relatives and friends at home. Of course it was denied by MOD, but nevertheless the very name *Canberra* mentioned on the news must send all their hearts to their boots."

I knew instinctively that those words summed up my family's position. My mother would be tuning into the news regularly, so at least she would hear the rebuttal in due course, but I also knew that she, and my sisters, would be worrying. My mother later told me that she had indeed heard the report, and that it had been one of the longest nights of her life until she had learned it was untrue. But at the time, there was nothing I could do but write a flurry of letters to them all and dispatch them as quickly as I could. Whatever danger I faced, sometimes being very far away and out of touch with the people you loved felt like the hardest thing of all.

Things were getting serious. Me ready for lifeboat drills.

SEVEN

By 25 May, we were steaming away in the direction of South Georgia. After the intensity of the previous few days, it was something of a relief to be heading away from the heart of the war zone, and to have a break from the tension and fear. Our instructions were to discharge the casualties, and to collect troops from South Georgia, which had been retaken. By now I had long accepted that I was part of something so much bigger than me, and I just had to do what we were told to do. The days of customising my uniform with a pink tie felt a lifetime ago. However, sometimes it was undeniably hard, living on speculation and rumour, not knowing what was coming next and simply waiting for some information to filter down. This uncertainty is very much reflected in my diary entries. One day, for example, I record that we won't be sent back to the war zone. The next, it is looking likely. And two days after that, we are there again, back in San Carlos Water.

28 May: We have discharged most of our precious load of survivors and patients. They've gone to *QE2* – it was a very big wrench for us, but probably a very necessary stepping stone for them. We are setting off tonight back to the Falklands but I don't think we'll go in so far as before unless it's really safe. I've spent quite long enough inspecting P&O floor coverings at close quarters. I've done quite a bit of cutting and sewing in the past few days and that is always satisfying.

Yesterday for the first time Angela and I decided to cook a meal but we only have access to a hot press, not a proper cooker, so we used the slow cooking method and made the most delicious hot pot. We cooked it all day in a champagne ice bucket and threw everything in we could lay hands on. With the usual P&O irony we couldn't find any carrots so we had to make do with asparagus spears. The six people we fed all agreed it was the best meal they had had since we left Southampton.

30 May: It's Sunday again, the air is still full of buzzes. We've now heard that we're not going in tonight as expected. Everyone's attitude this time is different from before. Then we didn't know what we were going into. Now we still don't know, but we have a better idea of the alternatives. We know we could be bombed or sunk and the expression "to risk your life" has a very vivid meaning now.

I really don't want to get killed, sometimes I do imagine an Exocet coming straight in through my window. That frightens me but I would probably be dead before I got scared. Being trapped by fire in the bowels of the ship is a nasty thought. I noticed that during the air raids that it is very important not to be alone. I did try a couple of times to lie down in my cabin, but after the third time of throwing myself out into the alley way, I realised that I was not going to get any sleep and also that I felt better in the company of others.

I've been up to look at the sun deck once again. We've now got thirty general purpose machine guns in a line on both sides. When I first saw machine guns on the bridge it frightened me, now I feel a bit safer knowing that we have at least some capability of shooting down planes. To do so in cold blood still seems horrible but if they were trying to sink *Canberra* I'd have no hesitation in saying, yes, we must shoot and we will.

June 2: Well, we are now safely in Ajax Bay, inside San Carlos Water. I got dressed and got into bed. A pipe was made for all ship's company to go to emergency stations, but there didn't seem much point, so stayed put. It's desperately hot sleeping in all your clothes – your feet feel as if they will melt, so eventually I took my shoes off but kept everything else on, though I was sure we'd get loads of time if there's an attack so I wasn't too worried.

I was lying half awake and half asleep. Just before seven, wondering if it was light outside yet. Then out of the silence in the darkness was the most horrendous bang, very loud, very close, from the bulkhead. Oh my God, I thought, this is it, my worst fears fulfilled. It was too dark to see anything, I was expecting a hole in the bulkhead. After a split-second hesitation, I scrambled out of bed and got out into my alley waiting for the next shot. Nothing happened.

I crawled up the passage and felt for my torch which hangs in the pocket of my combat jacket by the door. I noticed a smell but it wasn't of smoke or debris. The penny started to drop. I put on the torch and to my simultaneous relief and dismay I realised what had happened. A half-gallon can of concentrated orange juice had exploded.

Reading this entry forty years later, I can feel the frisson of fear that I lived with constantly during those days. The last thing any of us wanted was to go back into a war zone. The day was foggy, which worked in our favour, making it harder for enemy aircraft to attack. All afternoon troops were unloaded with provisions and packs, but as dusk fell it was obvious there was still much more to do. The decision was taken that we should spend the night where we were in order to continue the disembarking process the next day. No one got much sleep that night.

3 June dawned clear and bright, the sunshine bouncing dangerously off our shiny white ship. We continued disembarking troops and provisions until finally, at 1800 hours, we were ready to withdraw. We had just 620 people left on board and 413 of those were P&O crew. We had hardly any provisions left for ourselves, but we were alive and our job

in San Carlos Water, of safely transporting and disembarking troops, was successfully completed for a second time.

Once we were out of Bomb Alley, we stayed nearby, but not so close that we were at serious risk of being attacked. We sailed around the waters at a safe distance for some days, waiting for our next order. A great deal was happening around us and this intense phase of the conflict was soon to reach a conclusion. But on 3 June, the Navy was continuing to pay a heavy price. War ships *Sir Galahad* and *Sir Tristram* were hit by bombs in Port Pleasant and LCU *Foxtrot Four* was sunk by Argentine aircraft. HMS *Plymouth* was damaged by an unexploded bomb and HMS *Glamorgan* was struck by a land-based Exocet missile. Major assaults on Port Stanley continued and casualties continued to arrive on *Canberra*. Life on board rolled on, a bizarre mix of surgeries, mealtimes and concerts. It was at times extremely frustrating. Too many empty hours were spent watching films or playing quizzes, in between turning to real tasks like treating casualties or crew. By now we all knew we would not be going anywhere before the conflict was over. By this stage, I don't think anyone would have wanted to, and there was also a feeling that the end of the conflict might be in sight.

The overall spirit of the P&O crew had shifted quite dramatically since we had set off from Southampton all those weeks ago. In the early days, people had focused on the extra pay they felt they deserved for going on such an extended and unscheduled trip. But now all the talk was of near misses and risked lives and of having seen active service. It was the idea of some kind of recognition that made sense, rather than financial reward. By this stage, talk turned to the possibility that we had all earned a medal for our service. We had certainly all been changed by the experience.

When the surrender came, at first it felt tentative. Hand-to-hand fighting on the ground had come to an end and the islands had been reclaimed. White flags of surrender were being raised by Argentinian forces and the Union Jack was once more flying over Port Stanley. While we waited to hear if the surrender had been acknowledged by the Argentinian government, we still feared the Argentinian air force. There was a residual fear that they might make a last-ditch stand. As always, we just had to do as we were told and so with many questions unanswered, *Canberra* was sent to Port Stanley to pick up thousands of Argentinian prisoners of war. We were to help transport them back to Argentina.

As we sailed, it felt as if winter were closing around us. From the outset of the conflict, there had been an awareness that when the Falklands winter arrived it would be difficult to wage any kind of war. The military had worked out early on that there was a relatively small window of opportunity to reclaim the islands, hence perhaps the haste of our initial dispatch. Now, sleet and snow started to fall and the air turned icy. As we loaded the shivering and exhausted-looking prisoners of war on board, we also knew that many of our own men, still on land, needed our help. Thousands of our troops had lived in cold and harsh conditions for three weeks on the islands, in the land push to reclaim them. But the POWs were our current task at hand. Looking at them, it was easy to imagine their worried mothers and siblings and partners back home, wondering what had happened to their boys. Many of them looked very young and scared just like many of our own men. The Geneva Convention expects that every POW should be medically examined, and that task fell to me. I didn't feel apprehensive about this. As a doctor, I had always tried to remain detached from politics and this was no different. A patient who needed attention was simply that, regardless of whose side they were on.

June 15: In the soft lighting of the fully carpeted William Fawcett room there are guards with machine guns directed towards the quietly swarthy crowds of Argentinian prisoners. They slowly filed through the room having their names and numbers recorded. They had already been disarmed.

We met *Uganda* this morning. It's always been oddly emotional when two sister ships meet. *Uganda* was chugging along very close to us. Lots of people came out on the rails and started waving madly. Little *Uganda* gave a blast on her funnel, and *Canberra* gave a huge blast back that echoed around the Sound. *Uganda* replied with a rather hoarser effort, plus black smoke, and once again we responded with a deep full-bodied boom. It brought tears to my eyes. I'm sure I wasn't alone.

We are now anchored off Port Stanley with its funny British old houses. So that's what it's all about.

As the surrender held, there was time to assess the losses. Eventually, it was established that 255 British military personnel had lost their lives, and three Falkland Islanders had died in crossfire. Of these, twenty-seven were men we had transported on *Canberra*. Argentina had lost 649 military personnel, 321 of these going down with the *Belgrano*. The Royal Navy had lost HMS *Sheffield*, plus five other ships. A total of 34 planes had also been lost and the cost to the taxpayer for the conflict eventually ran to £2.78 billion. War is never a budget option. The bill had been high in every sense. As well as the dead, there had also been many casualties. Some had minor injuries, but others had been wounded very badly, with life-changing consequences.

By carrying prisoners of war, we had now become a cartel ship and so were protected by international law. We sailed to Puerto Madryn to disembark our cargo of POWs on 19 June. Approaching the dock, there was a mounting sense of apprehension. We were acutely aware that we were an 'enemy' ship arriving into an Argentinian port. We did not know what to expect. There might be joy to have their combatants returned. In reality a nervous calm prevailed as we docked. No military band or streamers. No families or loved ones. There was just a small reception committee and a line of vehicles to take the POWs away. I felt a sense of sadness that it had come to this. Their failure was not something we felt triumphalist about. The coolness of the reception was palpable. We did not really relax until we had sailed back into international waters again, ready to set off again to collect the rest of the POWs from Port Stanley.

However, on 21 June, a different order filtered through to us in the medical department. We were not going to be transporting POWs after all. Instead, we were to collect some of our own troops, most of those we had brought out to the conflict, and take them home. On hearing this, I don't think there was anyone on the ship who didn't cheer, inwardly at least. Smiles began to reappear and the tension, present for so long, began to ease. There was still much to do, and many patients to treat, but the conflict was over and we were going home soon.

It took a few days to sort out who was coming home on *Canberra*. In the meantime, we remained busy in the medical department, treating the less severe casualties as they presented. The major casualties had been taken by *Uganda*, which had been the primary hospital ship. The day before our departure, I went to pay *Uganda* a visit.

June 24: Yesterday I went over to *Uganda*. The horrors of war were there for all to see. The ship floats in its own world, very far removed from *Canberra*'s business-like attitude, or rather, war-like attitude. *Uganda* floats in euphoria, surrounded by heartbreak. Only the relief of its patients, that they are alive, keeps the place from falling apart from tragedy. The patients are different from ours. *Uganda* took over the job we initially thought we would be doing. But the maiming that I witnessed there is horrible, just horrible, even to me who has a pretty strong stomach. For them this war will never end. Every moment of their lives, they will be reminded of it.

The embarkation of troops – amongst others, 3 Commando Brigade, whom we had brought out to the Falklands three months earlier – was completed by lunchtime. Shortly after, we were sailing for home. The feeling was wonderful, a mix of relief, adrenalin and celebration.

As the Captain wrote in his diary that day: "… on board the mood remains fairly euphoric, not surprisingly, but at present the celebrations are generally under control. It is not too easy, however, as we have in the ship something near 2,000 teenagers who have just won a war."

Underlying this feeling, there was also a sense of relief among the crew that we had survived. Of course, not everyone was so lucky. Looking round at the troops we were carrying home, we were aware that some were missing. As we settled into our return journey, which was going to take at least two weeks, the mood settled and sobered. Yes, we were triumphant and going home to what would no doubt be a wonderful welcome, but the shadow of loss, and what some of those young boys had seen, also had its place on the ship.

When we had loaded in Southampton, all those weeks ago, some of the troops had made jokes about the inclusion of a psychiatrist. But it would prove to be a wise decision. In 1982, Post Traumatic Stress Disorder (PTSD) had not yet been widely recognised, but, just because the feelings weren't given today's familiar label, that didn't mean they weren't there and in need of addressing. In the First World War, PTSD had been called shell shock. In the 1980s, it was known as battle shock. Many of the troops were suffering from battle shock and it was hardly a surprise. Some had seen their best mates in the army shot and killed and they were barely twenty years old. They had quite possibly killed people themselves. Hand-to-hand fighting had ensued on land as part of the push to regain the islands. It doesn't take a vivid imagination to understand that surviving that kind of life-or-death situation required accessing a part of oneself that a person rarely or ever reaches in a regular daily life. They had of course been trained for it, but there is a world of difference between doing something in an exercise and doing it in real life.

The psychiatrist, Morgan O'Connell, was very kind and watched over me as a junior doctor, as well as the troops. He was very approachable, so when I could see the distress that was overtaking some of these teenagers as the dust settled on the initial euphoria, I took the problem to him. After some discussion, it was decided I could lead some small group sessions giving anyone who wanted to a chance to talk about what they had seen, and how they were feeling about it. It wasn't called therapy, but termed decompression. Again, as with PTSD, the labels were irrelevant. It was simply something that was necessary. The sessions ran daily with about six people in each group. Afterwards, I would go and talk to Morgan, to discuss how it had gone. It felt a very worthwhile thing to be doing, and he was extremely encouraging, an approach I have always remembered when I have had people training under me. It was a formative experience for me and I was able to do it at least in part because, in terms of war experience, they felt I was their equal. We had all been to the war zone. I understood their risks, as in some ways they had also been my risks. It felt important to help – I didn't want the young men to get home, go down the pub and go a little bit crazy without having had some outlet to work through what they had been through.

Meanwhile, my diary reflects my longing to get home.

27 June: I'm quite worried that these two weeks are going to be the longest of the entire voyage. Counting down to our arrival at Ascension Island. Decent weather.

6 July: We're now on British Summer Time. Home gets closer all the time. Speed on, speed on, Great White Whale.

The mixed mood remained until a day or two before we were due to reach Southampton. Then all thoughts turned rather abruptly towards home. We had been away for eleven weeks. No one had had so much as a day off. Now we were about to be reunited with our loved ones and move onto the next stage of our lives.

I had no idea what that meant in practical terms. P&O had made it clear that they had no future role for me after our return. That felt a little harsh but was the uncertain life of a ship's doctor and I accepted it. Contracts for the junior doctor roles were not secure. I had always known that there were no guarantees of future employment. As we sailed into Southampton, with the sound of military brass bands reaching our ears, the port lined with the flag-waving and cheering public welcoming us back, I put all thoughts of the future to one side. I was happy just to be home. I was smiling and scanning the cheering crowds for a friendly face. Somewhere out there was my mother and my family, who had come to meet me.

The reunion didn't have to wait long. Before the ship had docked, I had seen my family in the crowd. There was my mother, looking thinner and frailer than I remembered. Janny was in bright pink and easy to spot, with her husband and my little niece. Penny was there too, and they were all waving and shouting. Then I spotted Judy, whom I hadn't expected, as she was still living in Bahrain. She had flown back specially. I waved and called back, words carried on the breeze, the sound of the Royal Marines band playing all around me. I threw my hat down to Judy, who caught it, beaming widely, and promptly put it on.

Today there would be endless bureaucracy, but then family were allowed straight on to the ship as soon as she was tied up. Judy was one of the first up the gangway, possibly because she was wearing my P&O hat, and suddenly there they were, all around me: the people I loved most in the world. After months of letters and secret fears that I had worked so hard not to entertain, here we were together again. I led them down to my cabin and welcomed everyone into what had been my home for the last three months. After we had all calmed down, I packed up the few things I had, and with very little ado, said goodbye to a few colleagues and departed.

Walking down the gangway, my bag in my hand, I felt an unexpected stab of nostalgia already kicking in for what I was leaving behind. The experience had been extremely intense, and I had formed deep bonds with many of those with whom I had served. The months at sea had included countless hours of boredom and moments of life and death. Some of those who had sailed out on *Canberra* had not returned with her. It was an awful lot to leave behind me in a matter of moments. But the time had come. I had hugged Angela and Rosie and said my farewells to Peter and my other colleagues. Every step took me closer to home, a place I had conjured up in my dreams and longed for intermittently since the day we had set off. As I stepped off *Canberra* onto British soil for the first time in three months, I looked about me and felt a mixture of relief and melancholy at the same time. I followed my mother and sisters through the jubilant crowds ready for the journey home, with a sense that an important chapter of my life was closing.

Disembarkation – ready to head home.

EIGHT

Within hours of leaving *Canberra* I was back home in my cottage in Chigwell. The speed of transition from life on what was effectively a warship to putting the kettle on at home felt slightly surreal. For close to three months I had lived and breathed *Canberra* and the Falklands conflict in a floating community that resembled a self-sufficient town. Now I was back in civilian life, at home with my mother, with my garden full of yellow flowers. I had no idea what was for lunch, let alone supper, or what time any of it would happen. I had no troops to speak to or patients to treat.

For the first week, I was caught up in the whirlwind of return, which was made more intense by the fact that my sister Janny had shown my letters to a journalist. As a result the *Sunday Times* wanted to publish a double-page spread documenting some of my experiences. That came out a week after I returned, and for a little while I was caught up in the excitement of that. I was invited to go on *Woman's*

Hour, together with the war artist Linda Kitson. I hadn't met Linda before, as she had sailed to the conflict on the *QE2*. The attention stirred by the publicity brought a flurry of letters from friends I'd lost contact with and who got in touch when they learned what I had been up to. But slowly the fuss died away. Judy returned to Bahrain and my mother started to hunt for a house of her own. For everyone else, life, briefly interrupted by my return, went back to its normal rhythm. But my life didn't have a normal rhythm. Slowly I realised I had to face up to the fact that I was home, with the next phase of my life stretching ahead of me rather blankly. I had no job to go to and nothing pencilled in the diary beyond a holiday to Greece with a girlfriend.

Not having a job didn't particularly worry me at first. I had been paid very well for going to the conflict and so money wasn't an immediate issue. After a long stretch lived in high tension with not so much as a day off, I didn't really want to do anything for a little while. I could have taken up some locum roles, while I thought about what to do next, but what I wanted most was some time just to stop. With the hindsight of forty years, I understand now that I had quite a lot to process. I had been to war. I had seen people I knew killed or maimed for life. I had lived with a level of fear for my life and for those around me, for a period of three months. There had been a great deal of uncertainty. I had sailed out on a ship loaded with the Parachute Regiments and the Marines, and we had made the return trip without some of those brave young lads. The Falklands conflict was the last war where men were buried where they fell, rather than being repatriated. I wondered now if those boys had known any more about what they had signed up for than I had. I hoped so. I could only imagine how their mothers, fathers, siblings and partners felt.

The return had been a jubilant and triumphant celebration, a wonderful return for most. But there had been losses, and those young men would never be coming home. Every single one of those men was a life lost, a life story that had taken an unexpected turn and been cut short. I was a little shaken by all of that. Realisations came slowly. One day, I learned – I can't remember how – that if I had died, the Ministry of Defence would have paid out a great deal of money to my family. After that I joked that I was worth more dead than alive. It might have been a joke, but it was also the truth. In due course, my will was returned by P&O. These were sobering things that served to underline the unusual turn my life had briefly taken. So I suppose I was doing some decompressing of my own.

A little while after we returned, I was invited to the Ministry of Defence to discuss my experience. They wanted some feedback on how I felt the military had performed. I went to Whitehall and spent an afternoon talking to them. They asked me some important questions. One was, "Do you think it is right that women are allowed to go to war?" which I answered with an adamant affirmative. They also asked me how I thought women would have performed if they had been sent ashore. I remember replying that it was less about gender, and more about their attitude and training. If a woman were adequately trained and wanted to go, she should be allowed to do so. I remember feeling quite privileged that they had asked my opinion on this very important subject. I had not been held back by my gender only because I was not in the Navy. Had I been in the Navy, I would not have been allowed to go to war. But the irony was, if I had been in the Navy, I would have been much better prepared to face war and its consequences. I would have been trained in war surgery and other aspects of military medicine. That made no sense to me. It wasn't until 1990 that Naval policy changed, allowing women to do almost everything on an equal footing with men. I have no idea if my words carried any weight, or whether it was simply the changing climate of public opinion that brought about the opportunity for women to serve equally with men.

Late in the conflict, everyone who went to the Falklands was told that they should expect a medal on their return. I had thought there would be a presentation ceremony arranged, but in due course I learned that medals would be arriving in the post. Initially, mine was sent to the wrong address. I knew everyone I'd served with was receiving theirs, but nothing turned up for me. My sister Judy worked out that it must have been misaddressed, tracked it down and went to collect it. It is a South Atlantic medal, with a rosette, which denotes active service, and has my name engraved on the circumference. I felt very proud to receive it, even if the method of delivery had been unceremonious. I wear it on Remembrance Day each year, and it immediately tells something of my story. It is recognition that feels important. We had all faced risk. Everyone in the 28,000-strong task force received a medal, and that felt appropriate. There were other honours too. Rosie was awarded an MBE and Rick Jolly an OBE.

The conflict changed the thinking at home in terms of the military. At the outset of the conflict, many voices had been raised asking why the UK was defending territory that lay 8,000 miles from British shores. By the end, the entire country was lifted by the success. Margaret Thatcher's popularity as Prime Minister soared, and planned cuts to the Navy and the Air Force were cancelled. The Falklands Conflict had been the biggest military battle the country had been involved in since the Second World War, and it had reminded everyone why the forces were important.

Letting go of the experience of the Falklands conflict at a personal level was a gradual thing. For some people who had been involved in the conflict in some way or other, it became and remained the key three months of their lives. I didn't want that to happen to me. I was determined that it was just a three-month period of my life and I didn't want it to define me. As the dust settled and summer turned to autumn, I took my planned holiday to Crete and reconnected with other friends. I also relished spending so much time with my mother, who had gone from a size 14 to a size 8 while I had been away, through worry that I would not return safely. I stayed in touch with some of the people I had served with and particularly those from the *Canberra* Medical Society, which was the only connection I retained with the Falklands conflict experience, since I was not ex-military or full-time P&O crew. But I also wanted to put the episode of the conflict behind me and focus on the next stage of my life. I needed to push forward, and, as Peter Mayner had so wisely advised me, build my medical career on land.

Prior to the conflict, I had been training to be a GP and nothing that had happened had changed my mind about this direction. To complete my qualification required me to accumulate a certain number of days working in supervised practice. In reality, this meant working as a GP but with someone available to oversee me or advise me on a decision if necessary. Some investigation revealed that my time spent at sea could be included and I now had enough hours to qualify. Peter was a senior surgeon, and I had worked many weeks under his supervision. It had been a very unusual GP training, and while there might not be much call for digging shrapnel out of patients in a surgery in Chingford, the time had been served. I completed the paperwork and waited, ready to make a huge fuss if my application were questioned. But I was duly declared to be qualified, issued with my practising certificate, and suddenly there I was, picking up the threads of a more ordinary doctor's life, ready for my first GP job in a local surgery.

Judy (right) and me. Eventually looking less identical.

NINE

My first job as GP partner was in a practice with three other GPs, based in Chigwell. I was the only female doctor, working three days a week. I was introduced to the senior partner by my sister Janny, who was registered there. I had approached the surgery before going to the Falklands, and now I was ready to join. The three existing doctors felt that having a woman doctor would add something to the practice, but that I was required only part time. That suited me fine. Immediately on joining, my list filled to bursting, suggesting female patients had been wanting access to a female doctor for a while. The reality of a general practitioner's life had not changed since my early training. While I felt welcomed and valued by the women patients, and enjoyed the patient-facing aspect of the work, it was essentially a lonely job. A GP worked on their own, seeing patient after patient.

I realised early on that, if I didn't fill my empty two working days with other activities, I would end up working five days a week at the practice. There were more than enough patients to justify that. I had always had an interest in gynaecology and family planning, and I decided to pick this up now. I went back to a clinic in Walthamstow where I had worked at a young people's family planning clinic. I also worked sessions at the local private abortion clinic. I felt that clinics such as these were a very necessary medical service that should be more widely available. The clinics offered advice on contraception, but they also offered judgement-free terminations of unwanted pregnancies. This was still a relatively controversial issue in the 1980s, more so than it is today in the UK. To give a little background, abortion had been illegal in Britain until 1967, and even after the Abortion Act was passed, it was permitted only in very particular medical circumstances, largely related to the health of the mother or the foetus. Two doctors were still required to agree that a woman could have an abortion, and it was still an area in which people could be very critical. Every now and then there would be groups of people gathered outside the clinic, protesting against the whole idea. The area was still shrouded in disapproval and shame.

What we offered at the clinic was the opportunity for women to take control of their bodies, without feeling judged, and that felt like important work. There was a sector of society who felt it was wrong, and that women shouldn't have access to terminations. Any GP can make a referral unless they have serious conscientious objections, and I felt that a woman in this situation needs more than just a standard service. I sensed the relief from a woman when she found that she was seeing a doctor who was sympathetic and non-judgemental. I felt I could do this well. I already knew from the women I had worked with that no woman ever felt good about having an abortion. I've never met a woman who is enthusiastic about it. I had worked in central London at the Marie Stopes clinic during my training in family planning, and this gave me an outstanding basis for excellent service delivery.

However, I would not have wanted to make a career exclusively in this speciality. But providing terminations is a necessary part of medical services. And an important part of my career. Abortion is a choice that needs to be available to women. Today, one in three women in Britain will have a termination before they reach the age of forty-five. Women's lives, often lived as full-time employees and mothers and carers, are complicated enough. The prospective mother is the best judge of whether she can manage the pregnancy.

Family planning, contraception and reproductive medicine is still something of a 'Cinderella' speciality. This does not make sense to me, as contraception and the absence of it affect everybody. Yet today, doctors are not routinely trained in contraception. The Pill had been a great revolution in birth control, but it is not right for every woman. Alternatives existed but were less well known. The coil (intra-uterine device) is a simple solution that is very effective, but a doctor must be trained to fit it. I became skilled in fitting coils and I also trained other doctors to fit them. I found that it is a satisfying practical skill and a worthwhile service to offer. Twenty minutes' effort for up to five years contraception. This is such a benefit for the right woman.

Around the same time, I also started going into schools, teaching young people about contraception. It is important to reach young people before they become sexually active. Mostly I spoke to classes of young girls, but some classes were mixed or made up just of boys. Men clearly also have a part to play in birth control, and the better informed the boys are, the more likely it is that accidental pregnancy will be avoided. To support my interest in family planning and taking the message to the classroom, I took a course at the City and Guilds on adult teaching; it was an interesting new dimension to my experience. Intent on broadening my experience as fully as possible, I also worked at a vasectomy clinic. This gave me the chance to spend time with the supervisor who would become my much-valued practice manager, Yvonne.

After three years of working in this way, Dr Helen Wagstaff, who had overseen part of my training as a GP, approached me to join her as an equal partner in her small practice in Chingford. The practice had been started by Dr Joan Harcourt Norris, in 1934, and so was well established. Dr Helen Wagstaff and her sister Joan Wagstaff, also a doctor, had taken it over in 1946. Dr Helen Wagstaff had been running it ever since, and by the time I met her she was managing her practice alone. The opportunity to work with her, a woman doctor whom I respected, was too good to pass up. It was also on my home patch, which was appealing. For many years Dr Wagstaff had run the practice from her own home, and she was still doing that when I joined her. It was a general practice run in an old-fashioned style, and I had found my training with her much less isolating than previous experiences. Surgeries ran from 8.30 to 11, and then during coffee we could discuss any complex medical issues the morning had brought up. Afterwards I would take up the house calls and she would visit any patients on her list who were in the local hospital. In her spare time she kept bees in her front garden, and her patients would regularly say hello when they passed by. In 1987, in preparation for Dr Wagstaff's plan to retire, I purchased a building on the other side of the road to her house, and had it adapted to function as a surgery. This happened to be just 500 yards from my old school.

The move to join Dr Wagstaff was to be an important milestone in my career. I was to remain as a GP at this practice for twenty years. During this time, I would marry, have two children and grow into an experienced GP.

I was pleased to feel that I was finding my feet as a GP. I was feeling settled and found the work rewarding. Being a GP also had some advantages in those days. One of them was the ability to tailor the workload to other commitments. This made it more compatible with family life than many other medical careers. The option of working in a hospital or as a consultant did not offer the same flexibility at the time.

Two years after I joined the Chingford practice, I became pregnant with my first child. Dr Wagstaff said she would postpone her planned retirement until I had had the baby and was able to return to work. This was a generous offer and I was grateful. However, plans can and do go awry and this one did, albeit in a positive and happy way. I returned to take morning surgeries when my daughter was three months old, and around the same time I found that I was pregnant again. The result was that soon I had two children under the age of one.

In many ways this was less calamitous than it sounds. There is no easy way for a working woman to get through the early years of parenthood, and at least I got through the baby stage in fairly record time. Childcare was simplest to resolve by having a nanny to care for both babies at home. We quickly fell into a routine. I would run an open morning surgery each weekday before getting home for lunch with the children. In the late afternoon I would run another by-appointment surgery from around 4 to 7pm, before getting home to say goodnight. This gave me a chance to see my children on a regular basis through the day, which many mothers are not able to do. It also gave me time in the afternoon to pursue other aspects of my medical career.

When Dr Wagstaff retired, I became a single-handed GP. We also had a practice manager, a receptionist and a nurse. When Dr Wagstaff's existing practice manager retired, I recruited Yvonne, from the family planning service. We were a perfect fit for each other. A good practice manager makes all the difference to a GP's quality of life. I would not have lasted in the practice as long as I did had it not been for her.

It was a standard surgery set-up, and we offered all of the usual GP services. In those early days, appointment times were generous, and patients and doctors established an individual relationship. This had many benefits in terms of our diagnostic ability. Knowing a family's background and having some knowledge of the patient fed into our overall ability to work out what was going on for the patient and advise accordingly. I was joined by a partner, who embraced much the same values as I did as a GP. I trained her in the forensic work, and between us we were able to offer the Police a good service. We still needed our locums. She then left to return to hospital and academic medicine.

Being a GP is both an art and a science and I enjoyed it to a great extent. But I had long ago identified that I needed to develop other aspects of medical practice in order to keep me sufficiently interested and stimulated in medicine generally. I found the balance I required through family planning; as part of the medical team for the Royal Naval Reserve, which I joined a year after the Falklands War and as a direct result of my experiences in the conflict; and later as a forensic police doctor.

For this balance to work, I relied heavily on locums, and Yvonne, who was very good at organising them. She understood the importance of the other aspects to my career, and that, if I were to continue as a good local doctor, I had to regulate my time as a GP. Otherwise it was impossible to keep up with the intensity of the role. It is a very demanding job, with days spent fielding hundreds of questions from patients or from practice staff.

Over the years a good few locums passed through the practice doors. There was never a shortage of them as I clearly wasn't the only doctor who liked to diversify. However, we developed a working relationship with a couple of regulars who would come and work for us for a period, saving up their salary before going travelling for months at a time. This had the advantage of offering continuity for patients and the surgery.

For me, this mixed bag of medical experience proved successful for a long time, resulting in a varied and interesting career. However, during these years, numerous changes occurred in the daily life of the average GP and the tasks they were expected to perform. Administrative challenges ballooned and the numbers of patients each doctor was expected to treat and manage effectively also shot up. Appointment times shrank and then shrank again, until now they are a hopelessly optimistic nine minutes. In that time, a GP is supposed to find out what is wrong with a patient, prescribe accordingly, and record the details of the appointment in their notes. Little wonder, then, that today so many NHS GPs run late in their surgeries and eventually take early retirement. This latter choice was something that, in due course, I was also to opt for.

Back in uniform, this time as a Surgeon Lieutenant, Royal Naval Reserve.

TEN

By the end of 1982, just as I was settling into life as an ordinary doctor, I went to a Middlesex Hospital annual reunion dinner at the Savoy. I sat at a table with some of the consultants with whom I had worked as a junior house officer. One of these was Professor Roger Berry, who knew I had been in the Falklands. He asked me if I had ever considered joining the Royal Naval Reserve (RNR). He was a serving Captain with the RNR, and on learning this I understood why I had seen so little of him when I was his house officer. He had been working with the Navy doing medical research on submarines. As a specialist in nuclear medicine, this had clearly been a more important task than supervising junior doctors who would move on three months later.

I was interested in what he had to say about the RNR and remembered that Captain Scott-Masson had been a Reservist. I agreed to meet him the following week at HMS *President*, the ship on the Embankment that served as the headquarters for the Reserve. In the meantime I undertook a little background research into the Royal Naval Reserve, finding out that it was a part-time force made up of civilians, with around 3,000 members, offering a range of different skills in a Naval setting. As such, if I joined, it offered me the opportunity to be a part of the armed forces, while remaining a civilian and continuing my work as a GP. At least fourteen training days a year were expected at Naval bases around the country. It felt very much the kind of challenge I was seeking alongside my regular life as a GP.

I visited Professor Berry at HMS *President* as arranged and was shown around the ship and the sick bay, before going to have supper in the officers' wardroom. Another guest happened to be the First Sea Lord, Sir Henry Leach, and while I was still grappling to understand Navy hierarchies, I knew this man was very senior. I felt both privileged to be able to sit at the same table, and also competent to do so. I had seen active service, after all. The Navy does ceremony and entertaining very well, and by the end of the evening I was entirely won over. I had made up my mind: I would apply to join the RNR.

This decision was to open doors to one of the most rewarding aspects of my medical career and take me on any number of adventures.

My application was almost too easy. In those days I was not put through the challenge of the Admiralty Interview Board, which in later years became a hurdle even doctors had to leap. I was simply kitted out with uniform, appointed as an acting Surgeon Lieutenant and I was in.

As I lived about a mile over the boundary into Essex rather than London, I was sent to the Essex Communication training centre in Shoeburyness, rather than to HMS *President*. This was something of a surprise. I was too timid to question the decision, but I had heard that there were too many doctors at HMS *President*. I was slightly disappointed but duly turned up at Shoeburyness to find that no one was sure why they had acquired a doctor at all. They were there to learn about Naval control of shipping, from a variety of civilian jobs, so my experience, either Naval or medical, seemed of very little relevance. Nevertheless, I established a sick bay and tried to work out how to run it. I was available for medical consultations, and I was also responsible for carrying out the recruiting medicals. I soon discovered that Military Medical Classification is an art form that few understand, and in the absence of anyone being available to shed any light, I simply persevered and hoped that I didn't ruin anyone's military career – including my own.

Shortly after I arrived, the unit was commissioned as HMS *Essex* in due ceremonial, a formal event with full military pomp, to which I invited my mother. She was, of course, very proud of me.

I was sent to Britannia Royal Naval College in Dartmouth for my first annual training. This was enormous fun and a real learning curve. It involved a lot of outdoor exercises, including sailing, camping, marching and climbing, and certainly broadened my horizons. I also met other serving officers who were doing other courses, who had served in the task force to the Falklands. This was the first time this had occurred since the conflict, and I discovered how bonding that common experience was. It was as if we recognised something in each other, which meant we could share not just experiences but very deep emotions, even though we had only just met. It was an extremely unusual and powerful feeling and one that I've never forgotten. It still happens, when I go to ceremonies or events, and wear my South Atlantic medal, with the rosette that denotes active service. There will always be someone who will come over and start talking to me like an old friend, because they too were there.

After the training, I went to work intermittently as a hospital doctor at Stonehouse Naval Hospital in Plymouth. I would go down for a long weekend, or sometimes two weeks at a time, leaving a locum to cover at the surgery. It was an ordinary casualty job but one which felt collaborative and exciting. It was challenging to go back to hospital work but I knew I could fit into the system. Some tasks were harder than others. I clearly remember an old-fashioned red phone that sat on the desk of the casualty doctor's office. I was told that if it rang, it would be from someone calling from a vessel in the fleet who had a medical problem, and that whatever it was I had to deal with it. It didn't ring often, but if it did it would never be a simple question. Most ships had a Medical Assistant rather than a doctor on board and carried some medical supplies, but if they were calling it was because they were unable to deal with the situation that they were facing on board. I had to work out what the medical problem was and balance my advice, depending on the expertise of the caller and the needs of the patient. This somehow felt much more important work than simply picking up the phone in my suburban surgery. I was still an ordinary doctor doing ordinary daily doctoring, but everything had changed around me.

Working at the hospital, I often came into contact with people I had met at Dartmouth, and I felt welcomed and appreciated. In contrast to life as a GP, which is solitary at the best of times, doctoring in the Reserve was a much more collaborative experience. I was mixing with and meeting people who were supportive and wanted me to succeed, and who helped me to understand how the Navy worked. I quickly learned that I had to make my own luck. The memorable call that I had received from P&O, inviting me on my first cruise, would not occur in the Navy. Here, you had to make yourself visible, and work to be given the posting you wanted. Once I had found my feet and worked that out, I was determined to explore the extent of the opportunities available to me. Very early on I had ambitions to travel further than HMS *Essex* and, after a while, my determination to work abroad began to pay off.

In 1985 I was invited to HMS *Tamar*, which was in Hong Kong. I went for a month, taking special leave from my practice. It was a brilliant overseas opportunity. HMS *Tamar* was a tri-service establishment and I felt very comfortable doing that. I got to work with the RAF, which I hadn't done before. They flew me out to a ship and winched me out of a helicopter to do a medical inspection. This was followed by a trip in a Rigid Raider for lunch on a remote island. At the restaurant on the beach we chose live fish from the tank, which were cooked in front of us. And I was getting paid. A morning surgery in suburbia was no comparison.

In early 1986 I went on an Arctic training expedition to Norway with the Royal Marines. They taught me cross-country skiing and put me in for a competition. The Marines were doing it too, with huge bags on their backs. They slogged ahead of me totally uncomplainingly. I didn't have a pack, but when I got a blister on my heel, with some distance still to go, there was simply no giving up. It proved a small lesson on working through pain: I was so determined to finish that I just kept going. It gave me an understanding of the determination required by our forces, and that a person is much more likely to achieve something if they say, "I can do this" rather than "I will go as far as I can." On the same trip, I also spent a night in a tent at minus 35 degrees. I felt a little daunted, but it wasn't just me in the tent: I had five Royal Marines there too. There was no issue with the fact that I was female and they were male. It was simply an exercise and the men were happy to have a doctor with them, and they would not have let her freeze to death.

Interestingly, there was no fitness test required when I joined the Reserve, but it helped to be in relatively good shape. Fortunately, I was quite an active person, and I was only thirty-five.

As a doctor in the Reserve, I was first and foremost a doctor, but I learned many new things. I was willing to put my trust in the Marines or the Naval Reserve, and to embrace new experiences. I was always impressed by the spirit, organisation and camaraderie of the personnel, who were generally aged between twenty and late thirties. Most of the time when we were on exercise not very much happened, and I would sometimes feel that a nurse could have done my job just as well. But when something did go wrong the atmosphere would change dramatically, and I would have to step up and decide what happened next. One such incident occurred when I was working in a NATO base in Portugal. This was a shore-based medical centre and I was responsible for the fleet out at sea. I was invited to what seemed like a constant round of barbecues and dinners. It all felt very social, with little to no call on my medical skills. There was a very experienced practice manager who organised any routine medical appointments for me to keep, as well as focusing on my whereabouts every day and making sure I never missed a party.

As the days passed and I was shortly due to go home, I did wonder if I had done anything very much that trip to earn my salary. But that feeling changed in a heartbeat when a call came from a ship reporting a psychiatric emergency. At that point, the practice manager visibly threw his hands up, and stood back and deferred to me. Suddenly I was in charge. I had to decide what happened next. I was on my own. I arranged for the patient to be brought off the ship, and to be cared for initially on shore, and later flown home to appropriate care. That was one of the first times an event like that occurred, but it was far from the last, and really sums up what being a Naval Reserve doctor was like.

Almost all the time, nothing happened. But when things went wrong a specialist pair of hands was required. The possibility, however unlikely, that you might be called on in an emergency at any moment gave the work an unpredictable and demanding element.

In 1986 I did a locum role on RFA *Engadine*. Technically this was a merchant ship, so I was able to be the doctor on board. It was unusual for a female doctor to have previous sea-going experience, and perhaps this helped to qualify me. This time I was the only doctor on board, rather than being the junior of two. Most of the time there was little to do, but I took an interest in the helicopter training, and I was happy to spend the afternoons being winched on and off the deck in a Sea King helicopter. I was always completely confident that I would be looked after. As one of the officers said to me, "If you've only got one doctor, you are not going to drop her in the sea."

By 1990, when I had two small children, I avoided taking on long postings abroad. I was fortunate in that my family were very supportive. Undoubtedly the Reserve gave me something that other aspects of my career did not. Occasionally, when the juggling became too much, I would wonder if the time had come to leave. But my sister Judy would always encourage me to stay. She would remind me that I came back a different person after time spent with the Reserve: energised, alive and more dynamic, and that certainly reflected how it made me feel. So, I took her advice and kept going, even though at times it felt a real stretch. But those are decisions that mothers across the world face on a regular basis, and they are never easy ones to make when they require you to absent yourself for a stretch of time from your children's lives. However, my children never really seemed to mind. As they grew up they came with me to Remembrance Sunday services every year, and understood a little more of what it was their mother committed to when she went away from time to time.

While longer trips abroad might have been less possible when the children were small, I still took advantage of all the opportunities to do Naval training at weekends. These included Sea Survival, Aviation Medicine, Firefighting, Diving Medicine, War Surgery, Dentistry and Adventurous Training. I took everything offered. These weekends took place variously in Yorkshire, Scotland, Portsmouth and Cyprus, and after training I often put what I had learned to good use.

After my promotion to Surgeon Commander, I also served on the three aircraft carriers: HMS *Invincible*, *Illustrious* and *Ark Royal*. Working on board a ship as a doctor and an officer is unique. This sometimes called for different medical advice than might be appropriate for an identical condition on land. Each member of the crew had an essential job to do, so time off sick, which might be a reasonable treatment for the same problem in a civilian situation, was not an option. The emphasis was to keep the crew operational with minimal time lost. Equally, if a patient presented with a problem created by his behaviour, such as smoking or drinking, I could order him to stop. At home, I could only advise a patient with asthma that smoking was making it worse, and it would be a good idea to give it up. In the Reserve, I could instruct it. Similarly, it put an interesting spin on the doctor's obligation to confidentiality. If a patient had a condition that his superior needed to know about, then I had to inform them, whether the patient liked it or not.

I became the Principal Medical Officer on HMS *President* in 2004 and remained so until I turned sixty, when the rules meant I had to retire. It was with huge sadness that I stepped down, and my successor was to be the last PMO before the structure of the organisation was changed and the post ceased to exist. Of course, the structure of the Navy too changed over time – things always do. During my twenty-seven years, Naval hospitals closed and many tasks that had originally fallen to me and others like me were outsourced. But my twenty-seven years in the Royal Naval Reserve proved a very satisfying dimension to my career. So satisfying, in fact, that I worked as a recruiter for the RNR, talking to people considering applying and successfully encouraging doctors to join up.

With my mother at the Worshipful Society
of Apothecaries to receive my Diploma in
Medical Jurisprudence, 1992.

ELEVEN

The variety of challenges brought to my working life by my time as a Reservist underlined to me once again how medicine was a highly transferable skill that could take me into new places and situations. When I had become settled in my work for the Reserve, another opportunity presented itself. This time to work as a police doctor. This is now known as a forensic medical examiner.

In 1982 there was a disturbing documentary about Thames Valley Police that received widespread coverage in the press. Three male detectives interrogated a woman who had reported that she had been raped. Its brutality and cold-heartedness caused a sensation. The interview was later described as "possibly the most savage encounter between police and public ever recorded on television". The detectives involved were vilified. Thames Valley was the target, but the detectives had been taught this approach at Police College, and interviews like this were apparently happening everywhere. The documentary had a long-lasting impact.

By 1985, when I was established in general practice and was also working at family planning clinics and for the Reserve, it seemed an obvious next step for me to help women after an allegation of rape. I made some enquiries and it soon became apparent that many of the forensic examinations done after alleged rapes in East London were undertaken by one woman doctor at her surgery in Manor Park, which was not far from me. I contacted this Dr S. It turned out she was close to eighty, and considering retirement, and so she agreed in principle for me to take over. I applied to Scotland Yard and, following an interview, I was taken on.

Soon afterwards, I was called in the middle of the night to attend induction training. Dr S said very little to me, had a somewhat severe manner, and was quite off-putting, although clearly she was very good at the technical side of her job. She showed me how to collect the forensic samples and package and label them to go to the laboratory. She interacted very little with the victim of the allegation. After that single induction she retired and I was on my own, determined to be gentler and kinder than my predecessor.

I examined women at an examination suite away from the police station, re-purposed from the car pound. I quickly learned that to deal with a woman who has been traumatised and abused needs a very gentle touch. Research today shows that if a woman has a good experience, in terms of the necessary medical examination immediately after the event, the examination does not adversely affect her. However, if she has a bad experience with the examination, it simply adds to the trauma of the original assault. I never wanted to add to a woman's trauma. There has since been a great deal of media coverage on how the police treat victims of sexual assault, with the suggestion that it is not handled as sensitively as it should be. The police officers I worked with were almost always women and I found them kind and supportive. We worked well as a team to provide a service to women in need. It is clearly important that women get the treatment and support they need in these circumstances. I have always found that an open-ended approach to questioning and a kind and non-judgemental stance is the best way to help a woman explain what has happened.

I never knew what to expect when I was asked to examine someone. Once I was called in to examine a woman after an alleged assault. She had discovered clear fluid between her thighs and was convinced she must have been sexually assaulted in the night by an unseen intruder. I quickly worked out that her discovery was because she was pregnant and now in labour. She had had no idea she was pregnant and was shocked to find she was now 6cm dilated. I called an ambulance to the maternity wing of the nearest hospital. The officer in charge of the case nearly fainted with disbelief, and so did the soon-to-be mother, who gave birth to a healthy baby three hours later. It is incredibly rare in forensics to be able to give a cast-iron diagnosis, and this was one of the very few times I managed it.

Two years later, another media scandal was to lead to the expansion of my work as a forensic medical examiner, to include examining children in cases of abuse. In 1987, extensive media coverage was given to the Cleveland child abuse scandal. Following the introduction of a new technique by two consultant paediatricians to diagnose sexual abuse in children, Cleveland saw a huge rise in the number of children removed from their homes on grounds of sexual abuse in that year. Some 121 children were taken into care or kept in hospital wards. An inquiry the following year found that most of these diagnoses had been incorrect, and more than ninety children were returned to their homes.

As a result of that there was a shortage of doctors willing to be involved in such cases. In view of the fact that I was already working with the police, I was prepared to do it.

I started to examine children frequently, undertaking joint evaluations with consultant paediatricians. In many cases, the conclusion was that there was no conclusion. Many forms of sexual interference leave no signs. But if a doctor does not have the skills to look, the chance to collect evidence is lost. It was challenging work. The consultant was the specialist, and I was just the ordinary doctor the police had sent. I appreciated working with specially trained police officers, and we learned much from each other. I would give talks to police officers and social workers about my approach to examining small children. This included how important it was to give the children as much self-determination as possible; how I would sometimes sit on the floor to talk to them at their level; and above all, how important it was to convince the parent that bringing their child to the police in the first place was the right thing to do. I would deliberately not read the case notes prior to gathering physical evidence so I could form an impartial opinion. When a case involved a small child, a huge amount of patience was necessary. Sometimes more than one visit was required before it was possible to work out what was going on with a child. Two- or three-year-olds tend not to tell you things in direct ways. Once, I went to examine a little girl, and she sat under the basin in the consulting room and refused to come out. I had to come back the next day when I finally managed to persuade her to let me examine her.

I got to know the specialist police team at the East London police station very well over the years. They would call me at the practice or at home at night when they needed me to do an examination. I would almost always be able to oblige. However, on one memorable occasion, they phoned the practice to ask me to do an examination, only to be told by my practice manager that I was not available. The officer insisted, saying that she had seen me at a talk just the previous week, and wanted me for the job. My manager then said I was in the midst of labour. The officer reluctantly agreed that, all right, it could wait until after the labour was finished. It was only when my manager explained that I was having the baby myself did the officer concede that I really was unavailable this time. The officer must have gone away and wondered how he had missed the fact that I had clearly been nine months pregnant when he had seen me the previous week. Shortly afterwards came a big bunch of flowers with a note saying, "Never keep a secret from the police."

Friends often asked me how I could work with abused children when I had children of a similar age myself. To me this served only to underline the value of the work. My children were lucky enough to have a safe and loving home. Not every child is so fortunate. I did at times have to remind myself to step back emotionally, but detachment is a skill that doctors learn early on to survive in any kind of medical field. Any doctor will see much that is potentially upsetting in the course of a medical career and needs to be able to re-frame it as "How can I help here?" rather than "This is horrific, I can't cope." That kind of reaction might have sometimes been close, but professionalism always kicks in.

Intermittently, I attended courses run by Scotland Yard on aspects of forensic medicine. They offered the courses periodically, each time covering a different subject. This felt supportive and gave me a chance to meet other doctors working in the field. One of the benefits of the work was that it made me a better doctor in general practice. However, there were occasionally things I came across that went beyond my realm of understanding. One training session detailed self-harm in all sorts of variants and forms, and raised the question of when, if ever, piercings became self-harm. One of the examples they gave was of a man who had agreed to have his penis pierced. The lecturers then asked us to discuss whether that was a crime or not. This was beyond what I needed in general practice, but it meant that I was never surprised when I did routine medicals for the Navy.

In some ways my forensic work was a harrowing part of

my medical career. But it also felt useful and necessary and worth becoming good at. Keeping a calm exterior, whatever your inner thoughts, was essential. As with the Reserve, I learned that my responsibility as a forensic doctor was not just to the patient, but also to the police force and to the justice system. At times this was not without its challenges.

Early on in a forensic course, it was pointed out that doctors shouldn't believe everything the patient said. This flies directly against the training of a GP. A GP's job is to listen to your patient and believe them. As a forensic doctor, you are part of the chain of potential manipulation. Initially I felt quite concerned by the idea that I should not simply believe what the patient was telling me. I didn't want to take on a mantle of scepticism and stop believing what I was told. I had been trained that a good doctor listens and believes their patient. Fortunately, I was not often working with the person accused of the crime, but more usually the victim, and so it felt rare that I was being lied to. However, it is a jury's task to decide on the truth when two stories differ.

Nevertheless, there remained the awareness that I had to interpret what I saw before me, and what I was told. This was also in the full knowledge that, in due course, I might have to go to court and report my findings to a judge in front of a courtroom full of people.

Going to court was a natural extension of my work as a forensic doctor and something I had to get used to, both in the Crown Court and the Old Bailey. Public speaking was not something that came naturally to me and giving evidence was more complex than simply giving a lecture. I was giving evidence in open court, being stared at in a crowded courtroom, and I was expected to talk about injuries affecting the victim that, had they been reported to me in my GP practice, would have been treated as private and confidential information. It was often very personal medical information, revealed in minute detail, and it felt invasive of the patient's privacy. The idea of standing up in an open court, with the jury listening and barristers watching, and explaining injuries to a woman's vulva did at first feel inappropriate and against my medical teaching. However, it was simply a part of the job.

I also had to answer questions about what might have caused such physical injuries or effects. This was a fine balance between being a professional witness, documenting my findings, and being asked my opinion. Any misstep and the barristers could use it to discredit me. It took me a while to learn that while an expert forensic witness could generalise and pass an opinion on what might have caused an injury, I was a professional witness and could only say "This bruise is consistent with a blow being delivered three days earlier." I had to confine myself to the facts and cut myself off from the poor patient's embarrassment. This was made harder by the fact that they were almost always in the courtroom as well.

A style of communication that is normal in my consulting room is not necessarily appropriate to a courtroom. As a GP, if a patient doesn't understand what you are saying to them it is good practice to express the same idea in a different way. However, adopting this in court was, I quickly learnt, exactly what *not* to do. For instance, early in my career as a forensic doctor, I described a patient who was trembling as "looking anxious". The barrister immediately asked me to explain why I considered the patient to be "looking anxious". I said, "Well, she seemed agitated," and the barrister proceeded to grill me over the difference between the meaning of "agitated" and "anxious". "Which one was she?" he asked. After that, I very quickly learned to say "her hands were shaking" rather than to express my own thoughts on the meaning of the physical symptom. Let the jury do that.

It was a steep learning curve and the only way I coped was by not spending too long thinking about it. I had my notes and I avoided saying anything that I had not recorded in those notes: I stuck to the script, and I tried not to get myself into trouble. There was quite a lot of theatre involved, and the defence barrister's objective was to discredit me. But as with everything, it got easier with experience. On the first few occasions, I felt quite overawed and made notes, writing down the names of the judges and the barristers. However, as it became a more frequent occurrence, sometimes going about three or four times a month, it settled into just one more element in a day that could include a morning GP surgery, a trip to the Old Bailey in the afternoon, before an evening surgery back at the practice. I was delighted that one day could offer so much variation. I never spent an entire working day in the same location.

By 1989, I had become fairly experienced at appearing

in court. However, there was never any control over the timing of court appearances. Snaresbrook Crown Court is in Wanstead, and I could get there from my surgery in about twenty minutes. The Old Bailey was trickier, requiring a drive and then a trip on the Central Line. The journey door to door took about forty-five minutes on a good day.

Despite this, I was hardly ever late. The officers in charge of the case would help me with the tight time schedules as much as they could, as would my practice manager by heading off any extras during the morning surgery. The most problematic times came when I was breastfeeding. I was reminded of this recently, when the MP Stella Creasy objected to not being able to take her baby into the House of Commons. Many women return to employment while still breastfeeding and enabling them to do so while attending a place of work seems to be an ongoing issue that was unaddressed in my time. Shortly after I had my second child, I was called to the Old Bailey to give evidence. Initially I said I couldn't go, as I had a five-week-old baby. Of course, they insisted that I attend. I asked for someone to look after the baby. I was told there was a matron on the premises who did first aid but not childcare. It wasn't the most helpful response. Still, with little choice I set off, feeling rather vulnerable to be taking such a small baby on the tube. I arrived, and waited two hours to be called, before being told that the case had collapsed and I was free to go. I felt a mixture of relief that I didn't have to abandon my baby, and irritation that I had been dragged there at all.

I hope the system has changed today to become more

accommodating to breastfeeding mothers. Perhaps giving evidence by video link is an option in these more advanced technological times, and one would hope there would be provision of a mother and baby room as standard. Still, as Stella Creasy's recent battle showed, it isn't safe to assume these changes have happened.

Once I had adjusted to the demands of giving evidence, I decided to take the Diploma in Medical Jurisprudence. There was no organised course for this. It was a case of studying the syllabus at home and presenting for examination in due course. With two children under two it was an additional workload to fit in, but what I learned was fascinating. In all my history of education, never had I found study so immediately applicable to my everyday working life. I liked the idea that I would study something in the afternoon that I might have to put into action the next time I was called to a police station. That was a motivation to keep going, as it was a tough course and a difficult exam. But I learned a lot and was pleased to have done it. Indeed I became very interested in custody work as well as victim assessment.

I dug deep into the job of being a forensic doctor and it was a hugely satisfying aspect of my career. It was work I considered to be important and a contrast to my GP practice, where everything was slow and steady. Things that go wrong for people who present at a GP are all variations on similar themes. The same conditions present again and again. In forensic work, each case is an absolute one-off. In forensic practice there is time and space to deal with it effectively. As a GP, to be able to spend even an hour considering one case was unthinkable, even in the 1980s. In general practice the expectation was that you saw the patient, made the notes, prescribed pills or treatment or wrote the referral letter, all in about twenty minutes, before moving on to the next patient. But dealing with an allegation of rape or the sexual abuse of a child, it was understood that a doctor had to spend as long as was necessary with the woman or the small child concerned. These types of patients have been through something shocking and traumatic, and they need to be given the time and attention required to ascertain correctly what has occurred, while at the same time giving them the care they need as individuals.

As a forensic doctor, police station work brought me into contact with a very different section of the public, one that I didn't see at my GP surgery. On a typical Saturday night, many of the people I treated had drink or drug problems, which were fundamental to them ending up in custody. Up to this point, I had had very little experience with drugs. It was still the 1980s and drugs were less in evidence than they are today. It was a new challenge, and there was a certain conflict to it. While my instinct told me that I wanted to help the person in question to get off drugs that were clearly doing them no good at all, the reality was I was there only to assess and treat them in that moment. I had no remit to consider further treatment, which made me feel that I was just the temporary fix. Too often I simply had to prescribe methadone, which made me feel that I was supporting their habit. Now that has changed and for the better. There is much more focus on harm reduction, and the medical profession and society is much more aware that turning people with addiction problems into criminals is rarely helpful.

It was also more complicated treating a patient who had taken drugs than one who had not. Drug use can mimic symptoms and affect behaviour in a way that distorts the picture of a pre-existing disease or condition. For example, if a patient was slurring their words, it was important to determine whether they were doing so because they were drunk or had taken a substance, or whether it was because of some underlying health condition. Getting that kind of decision wrong could potentially end a doctor's career. It was a heavy responsibility, but it probably made me a better GP.

At the Falklands War Memorial in London.

TWELVE

By 2003, I had been a qualified doctor for twenty-five years. During that time, the profession had changed hugely and many medical advances had been made in terms of saving lives and creating new ones. However, the administrative changes in the supportive structure of the NHS did not always come for the better, from the point of view of either doctors or patients. This was to be a key reason why I would take early retirement from general practice. But, before I reached that point, I took the decision to stop working as a forensic doctor.

The reasons were twofold. The first was practical. By 2003, examinations of alleged victims had been centralised, and the journey was much further from where I lived. I spent longer in the car, battling through London's infamously bad traffic, and that didn't make the demands of the job any easier. Many of the calls came in the middle of the night, and if I was away too long that had an effect on my ability to hold daily morning surgery. However, what really brought me to the decision to stop working as a forensic doctor was something more serious and beyond my control.

It came about through one case. In this instance I was called to the Old Bailey to give evidence in the prosecution of a man accused of rape and assault. I had examined the victim some months previously and had duly reported the findings of my medical examination to the police. The Crown Prosecution Service had reviewed the evidence, including my medical evidence, and had decided to prosecute the accused. Nothing of this was unusual. At the height of my work as a forensic doctor I was giving evidence frequently and this was simply one more case, and I took it as seriously as I did all of them. I gave my evidence, seemingly without mishap, and sat down again. At no time did I think anything out of the ordinary had occurred. The court was full of the usual people – the accused, his legal team, the jurors, the judge, plus a handful of curious people sitting in the public gallery. The accused was found guilty, which was not a surprise to me, and given a prison sentence. And that, I mistakenly thought, was that.

Unfortunately the accused thought differently. Locked up in prison with time on his hands, he started to write a series of complaining letters. One of these letters was sent to the General Medical Council and concerned me. In it he stated that I had been prejudiced against him. When I first heard this I was astonished, but not unduly concerned. There was no evidence or reason that he offered to support his claim and none existed. I fully expected the GMC would dismiss the issue. I was simply a professional witness doing my job, while he was a convicted rapist. Eventually, the GMC did dismiss it. But they took two long years to do so. During this time they investigated his claims, before finally saying, without any hint of apology to me, that there was clearly no case to answer.

The strain of this two-year wait took a considerable toll, and I decided it was time to bow out of forensic medicine. My commitment to my profession, like that of most doctors, is very deep, but when dented by this experience I felt the only safe path was to withdraw from an aspect of medicine that had left me so vulnerable.

I handed in my notice. My fifteen years of working with the police came to an end without fanfare. I was simply there one week and gone the next, without so much as a goodbye card. It had been a curious chapter in my professional life, and despite the way it concluded I don't regret it one bit.

Two years later, in 2005, I also took the decision to resign from my practice in Chingford. By this time I had been in general practice for close to thirty years. The NHS had been in stress when I had joined it in 1978, and during the years I had been practising it had become a service in crisis. Underfunded and understaffed, it was much criticised by the press and the general public. Every day was a case of trying to do too much on too little. A doctor walked a complex tightrope, balancing the demands of the state and patients, who grew ever more demanding.

When I started at the Chingford surgery, at the age of thirty-five, we had 1,800 registered patients on our list.

Today, at the same surgery, which has not moved facilities, there are approaching 8,000 on the list. The premises are not big enough to have that number of patients, or to meet their needs with only three full-time doctors. Inevitably there has been a knock-on effect to the service the doctors and the surgery are able to give. It is simply not possible to ask for more to be done with the same resources in the same time and space without a detrimental effect on the patient. This is what GPs were and still are asked to do. During my years as a GP, the changes in general practice were multiple. Many changes depersonalised the job. The burden of chronic disease management rose, the patient expectation was continually being raised higher with new services introduced, and the administrative load was on an ever-upward march. Everything needed to be measured and the boxes ticked, and it felt increasingly as if I were an operative rather than an advisor or advocate. The result was that I became so demoralised that I decided to step back.

As a society, we are moving to a point where we understand that unrelenting pressure does indeed affect people, and that the mind and body do not act independently of each other. Stress cuts short lives and causes all sorts of problems of its own. But this is still a relatively new acknowledgement. Much like the fact that the term PTSD was not widely used until the 1980s, so the issue of workplace stress was slow to be recognised, most of all perhaps by the very individuals suffering from it. We were, until recently, a nation famed for our 'stiff upper lip' qualities, and it would take a pandemic for mental health to become as widely talked about as the common cold. Doctors are generally very committed to serving their patients, and it was very hard to walk away after many years of practice. I have always hated to let my patients down. On one occasion, some years earlier, I ran a surgery while in significant pain from a complication with my second pregnancy, at the end of which the practice nurse drove me to hospital where I stayed for several days. In 2005, I was just as reluctant to leave them.

At first, I hoped that a break from general practice would be enough to revive me. I took some time off, before resuming some work as a locum. This last experience was what made it abundantly clear to me that general practice had changed too much for me to find my place in it again. At the age of fifty-five, I left the surgery for the last time, departing from quite a different job to the one I had started many years previously.

The space this left in my life gave me time to go back to sea briefly, as the surgeon on RMS *St Helena*. This allowed me to return to Ascension Island. Having spent so many days sailing round it in 1982, it felt very special finally to go ashore.

I also spent more time with the Navy, serving on all three of the aircraft carriers and in shore-based medical centres. It always felt a great privilege to be accepted so readily into such a specialised world.

As a rule, I have actively chosen throughout my career not to engage in the politics of a situation, but to focus on the treatment that the patient in front of me requires and deserves. Thus it was in the Falklands, when a prisoner of war was as deserving of proper medical care as our own forces. Similarly, with my work as a forensic doctor and in family planning, I focused on remaining objective about the patient rather than getting involved politically in the rights and wrongs of a situation. I am first and foremost a doctor and a huge believer in the NHS. I have spent my entire career within it and never had an interest in developing any kind of private practice, even though the pay is better and it has kinder hours. I had been brought up on the NHS and that was where I wanted to work. However, even an ardent supporter like me can see that today's NHS is a service at a crossroads, and some fundamental decisions need to be made. Staff are exhausted and demoralised, and patients are being failed. The NHS is working very hard to emerge from the pandemic years and to grapple with the longer-term problems it faces. Although some of those problems have been in existence for a long time.

Some might legitimately wonder how such a dazzling idea as free healthcare for everyone resulted in what we now have today, but a look at the origins of the NHS reveals that it isn't as unlikely as it seems at first glance. The NHS started life in 1948, a positive national development following hard on the heels of the end of the Second World War. No other country in the world had attempted a completely free national health service before. It had been some years in the planning, and it was and is a noble idea, but it was beset with challenges from the beginning. The service wasn't a brand-new service, as perhaps many people assume, founded on new facilities. It was a brand-new concept, but it was built precariously upon a range of previously existing facilities, including cottage hospitals, independent general practitioners and myriad charitable foundations, which were pulled together and placed under an umbrella marked NHS, in an attempt to unite them into a single service. Unsurprisingly, there were problems from the outset. The Second World War, only three years in the past when the NHS was formed, had highlighted the shortfall in various aspects of medical care that the existing services were providing. One of these areas was hospitals. There was also war damage to medical facilities – every single hospital in London suffered some element of bomb damage. Following the end of the war, there was also a chronic shortage of nurses. So, from the outset, the system was understaffed and under-resourced, and that is a situation that continues today. This is evident across the NHS, from the demands placed on the individual GP to overworked junior doctors in hospitals.

In the seventy years since the NHS was created, the scope of medicine and what it can do has changed hugely. What we can treat, what we can prevent, and what we can protect against, have all expanded and, of course, that is to be celebrated. Today, it is unlikely that someone in the same situation as my father would die at fifty-two. Medical advances might have prevented his fatal heart attack from ever happening. The anti-smoking measures introduced some years ago would have encouraged him to quit, and the range of modern treatments available would have ensured he saw all his daughters grow up.

Life expectancy has grown by thirteen years for men since 1948 and twelve years for women, which throws up a whole host of new conditions stemming from a longer period of old age that require time-consuming and costly treatment and management. There is so much more that medicine can do that not only contributes to the workload crisis doctors currently face, but also gives rise to the still unresolved issue of when it becomes the wrong choice to intervene. Patients now routinely sign 'do not resuscitate' orders, and prepare living wills, to avoid being kept alive when it is technically and medically possible, but not in a state in which they wish to exist. A person's right to die is still a hotly debated issue, with a private member's bill currently working its way through the House of Lords legislative process. It is a valid question that needs to be pursued further. Back in 1948, when the NHS was conceived as a diagnostic and treatment service, nothing of this dilemma could have been imagined. It was a service all about saving lives.

Today that means there is an emphasis on prevention as well as treatment. Prevention can be hugely effective but the responsibility for it falls to primary care and the GP in the first instance. It takes time to deliver, and time is something that doctors are increasingly short of.

Patients and their expectations have also changed. In 1948, the average patient felt extraordinarily grateful to see a doctor at all, and not to have to pay for it. Prior to the NHS, families had to fund any medical care. Most could not afford that, which meant that people were in the habit of going to the doctor only if they really needed to. The responsibility to look after their health fell on their own shoulders. By 2022, this responsibility has in part at least shifted onto the doctor. It is unrealistic to assume the NHS can take all the responsibility for the 'fix'. People need to continue to take responsibility for themselves and, while there is a growing acceptance of this, health advice doesn't always reach those most in need.

When a health message is reinforced by Government-backed policies, the results are seen more clearly. Smoking was widely known as a serious risk to a person's health from the 1960s. Yet it wasn't until smoking was banned indoors, and it was essentially made very hard to smoke, that the numbers of cigarette smokers declined dramatically. Fewer new smokers took up the habit, leading to a gradual decline in numbers of smokers overall. The number of people who have never smoked has increased from 37.4 per cent in 1974 to 60.4 per cent in 2019 (according to ASH).

The mood within the NHS today is one of despair. Every encounter I have with younger doctors, at medical conferences, and at lectures, reveals that the NHS, the healing service we all rely on, is itself wounded. Almost every doctor I speak to is looking for a way out. We also have a staff shortage, particularly of nurses. Part of this despair comes from the fact that patients are being failed. An estimated one in nine people in the UK is now on an NHS waiting list, and some of these lists are years long.

The NHS employs 1.3 million people (NHS Providers) making it the largest employer in the country and the most expensive drain on the taxpayer's funds. In the year 2020/21 it cost £192 billion (The King's Fund). That represents 10.2 per cent of GDP spent in an attempt to meet the health needs of every person in the country. On an average day in the NHS, 1 million people will attend a GP appointment, some 250,000 people will attend an outpatient's appointment, more than 30,000 people will call an ambulance, and 45,000 will attend A&E. Despite the problems that beset it, the NHS is clearly still working very hard. The problem is that it just can't deal with the challenges it faces as things stand. Making the situation even worse, demand is always on the increase: in 2019, there were 1.7 million more attendances at A&E departments than in 2011 (The King's Fund). In addition to day-to-day demands, with an increase in life expectancy and many more diseases that can be treated but require regular care, the calls on all aspects of the service have risen.

The NHS has to face reform if it is to survive. But any change must be the *right* change. It must be the change that brings about what we are all seeking: doctors and nurses who want to stay in the service, and patients who feel they can access a doctor and get the treatment they need within a reasonable time frame.

The problem of lack of staff facing the NHS is a complex issue. At one end, it starts with its newest recruits, many of whom have already decided they want to leave the profession by the time they graduate. In many ways this is unsurprising given the challenges the service faces. Working in the NHS is always going to be highly challenging. With many young people signing up for medical school at the age of eighteen with little or no hands-on experience of the service, some have no real idea of the career choice they are making. Applicants to the four-year fast-track medical training scheme, which is open to graduates with a first degree in a different discipline, generally have a much greater understanding of what they are getting into. In my experience, training as a doctor as a more mature student had its advantages. Accepting eighteen-year-olds into medical schools and turning them into doctors may no longer be appropriate. This view is reinforced by my time spent on the interview boards of a London hospital for applicants for the four-year course. Every applicant to this course had come to medicine more slowly, almost in spite of themselves, and was hugely committed to it as a career choice. As well as having taken their first degree in another discipline, they may have worked in a hospital laboratory or in the ambulance service, for example, and seen first-hand what they are getting into. Consequently, the retention rates of doctors who enter medicine through this route is much higher than for those who embark on a medical degree at the age of eighteen. However, the acceptance rate through the graduate route is just one in four applicants. So there is a huge pool of suitable candidates who could be fast-tracked into becoming doctors.

Looking at the staffing crisis from the other end of the experience spectrum, I was surprised during the pandemic that as a retired doctor I was not invited to help at vaccination centres or in any other way that contributed to the effort to keep the NHS operational, despite being given temporary registration by the GMC. As a retired doctor, I would have been perfectly happy to work under the supervision of a younger doctor, and to explain to patients that I had come back out of retirement to help in the crisis.

It is also worth noting that if it were less difficult to work part time, fewer doctors might opt for early retirement. The GMC currently makes it difficult for older doctors to retain their medical licence when they are planning to work only part time. Clearly all doctors have to be held to the latest standards, but when the cost to remain qualified is far greater than any part-time earnings, and the hoops required to jump through so frequent, this is genuinely off-putting, and so considerable talent, with years of valuable experience, is lost.

The recent pandemic had been predicted for many years. When it hit us in March 2020, as a nation and a health service we were not ready. Looking ahead, to avoid such pressure occurring on the NHS again, perhaps creating a system of reservists, much as the Navy does, might enable us to be better prepared. With a small investment in training each year, a retired force of doctors, nurses and other medical staff could be maintained, and called on in the event of the NHS possibly becoming overwhelmed. NHS-trained doctors and nurses and other medical staff are very highly regarded. The training is extremely good. Once that investment in training has been made, we need to encourage all possible ways for people with varying demands on their time to be able to remain in the profession and in the NHS as long as they possibly can.

Today's GPs are working harder than ever, in a service that actually receives just 9 per cent of the NHS budget (BMA, 2021). Many GPs are at work every day from 7.30am catching up on mountains of paperwork before seeing patients, and don't finish their working day until 7pm or later. There is less time and more to be done than when I started; little of the family-friendly hours that I enjoyed and far more administration. This erosion of time is a key problem. Being a good doctor does require time. Today's short appointments mean a doctor has to quickly deliver an outcome and move on to the next patient. There is little time for the listening that underpins good doctoring.

A great deal is expected of GPs today. One current focus of mine is on helping other doctors and medical students as they come through the system that so supported me. Grants made my own training possible, and in turn I, in my own small way, try to sponsor medical students in financial hardship. I have also recently become a trustee of the Royal Medical Benevolent Fund. The fund works to support doctors in financial difficulty. Many doctors have lost jobs or have found the stress of expectations too much. Much will be heard of this situation in the future.

I am also a Fellow of the Medical Society of London, which was founded in 1773 and is a forum for doctors to share academic aspects of and developments in medicine. Doctors have been committed to high standards long before our performance was as closely monitored as it is now. Most of the Fellows are specialists in their fields. There are also a growing number of ordinary doctors like me.

General practice is the cornerstone on which the NHS is built, and the GPs of today and tomorrow need to be supported if they are to continue to be the starting point of all healthcare for the nation. To attract them and retain them, they need to be able to have the same kind of rewarding career that I had. In turn, every patient will benefit.

EPILOGUE

I turned to medicine because I wanted to care for people, and most young people who choose medicine today do so for the same reason. As a newly qualified GP, I set out to approach the issues that patients had with sensitivity and to diagnose and treat them. I wanted to be like Doctor Mac. *An ordinary doctor*, helping the patient in front of me.

Doctor Mac was valued by my family. We felt that he was looking after us. He was not a mere 'service-provider' or a 'gatekeeper'. Both he and Dr Wagstaff nurtured personal connections with patients. When I worked in Chingford, a few hundred yards from where I went to school, I felt that I had turned back in time. This was general practice from a different era, and patients valued the fact that I was an ordinary girl from the local area.

But what does it mean to be an ordinary doctor? I was aware early on in my career that some doctors were put up on a pedestal. I remember saying to myself that I did not want to be a 'pedestal doctor'. For me, the ordinary part of being a doctor has involved being as approachable as any other person. I was working collaboratively with patients long before it became the accepted approach to a consultation. I guarded my privacy closely, but patients were thrilled when they found out that I too was living my life, having a family…

Perhaps no doctor's life is completely ordinary because we are given the enormous privilege of being holders of information. Training gives us access to a huge body of knowledge. Of course, patients can also easily access information, but the ability to process that data and apply it to an individual is something that doctors learn, and it goes way beyond the best algorithms, which is why I believe that human doctors will always be needed, despite the progress of IT diagnostics. We also hold a quality of information about patients impossible to record on a computer. We see the look on their face when they part with a piece of information. We respond to that, not just to the words. This is a very great honour to share. Doctor Mac never wrote anything at all in his notes, but he was treasured by his patients. He was an ordinary doctor doing the job in his own style.

I now think that I was indeed an ordinary doctor, and I never did climb onto that pedestal of the all-knowing expert. I was always ready to revise an opinion, acknowledge the unknown and refer a problem to specialists. I think and hope that my patients valued this. Times, of course, have changed, patient expectations have evolved and they are less likely to accept uncertainty. Patients now tend to link uncertainty with incompetence.

I appreciated the help I had from other doctors and I continue to give similar support to younger colleagues. I fear that their challenges are greater than mine were. Pressure to be one hundred per cent correct in every consultation weighs, so perhaps the era of the 'ordinary doctor' has drawn to a close.

Acknowledgements

I would like to express my thanks to the following:

My cousin Mandy, who first got me talking about my story.

My sisters, who always cheer me on whatever I get up to.

My dear friend Nicola, who always believes in me.

My practice manager Yvonne, without whom I would not have survived in general practice so long.

The patients who entrusted me with their needs.

My Naval colleagues, who always patiently explain the system to Reservists.

My police colleagues, who strive to do a good job.

My NHS colleagues, who continue to look after us all.

Mary Alexander, whose enthusiasm and skill launched me into the project.

Sam Carter for steering a steady course to our destination.

My daughter and son, who are my constant inspiration.